The ultimate Good ene

365 Days of Energizing Recipes with a 28-Day Meal Plan to Simplify Healthy Eating and Boost Your Well-being

Lisa Bestley

SUMMARY

Chapter 1: Introduction to Wellness Through Nutrition

In today's fast-paced world, where schedules are jam-packed and time is often a luxury, maintaining energy levels throughout the day is a common challenge. Many people struggle with fatigue, lack of focus, and fluctuating energy, all of which can severely impact daily productivity and overall well-being. The connection between what we eat and how we feel is profound, yet often overlooked. This chapter explores the crucial role that nutrition plays in sustaining energy and offers practical strategies for integrating sustainable, nutritious eating habits into even the busiest of lifestyles.

1.1 The Importance of Energy Through Diet

Energy is the foundation of our daily activities. Without sufficient energy, both our physical and mental functions suffer, leading to decreased productivity, mood swings, and a general sense of lethargy. The food we consume is the primary source of this energy, acting as fuel that powers every function in our bodies. But not all food is created equal—different types of nutrients provide varying levels of energy and affect our bodies in distinct ways.

Carbohydrates, proteins, and fats are the three macronutrients that supply energy to our bodies. Carbohydrates are often considered the body's preferred energy source because they are quickly converted into glucose, which our cells use for fuel. However, the type of carbohydrates consumed is critical. Simple carbohydrates, found in sugary snacks and processed foods, lead to rapid spikes in blood sugar followed by equally rapid drops, which can cause energy crashes. On the other hand, complex carbohydrates, such as whole grains, vegetables, and legumes, provide a more steady release of energy, keeping blood sugar levels stable and sustaining energy over longer periods.

Proteins, composed of amino acids, are essential for the growth and repair of tissues. They also play a role in the production of hormones and enzymes that regulate various bodily functions, including energy metabolism. While proteins are not the body's first choice for energy, they are crucial for maintaining muscle mass and supporting long-term energy levels, especially when combined with carbohydrates in a balanced diet.

Fats are another important energy source, especially for prolonged, low-intensity activities. Fats are calorie-dense, meaning they provide more energy per gram than carbohydrates or proteins. Healthy fats, such as those found in avocados, nuts, seeds, and fatty fish, are particularly beneficial as they support brain function, reduce inflammation, and provide sustained energy without the blood sugar fluctuations associated with simple carbohydrates.

In addition to macronutrients, micronutrients—vitamins and minerals—are vital in energy production. B vitamins, for example, play a significant role in converting the food we eat into energy that our cells can use. Iron is another critical mineral, as it helps transport oxygen throughout the body, which is essential for energy production in our cells. A deficiency in these or other key nutrients can lead to fatigue and decreased energy levels.

Water, though not a nutrient in the traditional sense, is equally crucial for maintaining energy. Dehydration, even at mild levels, can significantly impair cognitive function and physical performance. Water is involved in nearly every bodily process, including digestion, circulation, and temperature regulation. Ensuring adequate hydration throughout the day is therefore essential for sustaining energy levels.

A balanced diet rich in whole, unprocessed foods provides the nutrients necessary for optimal energy levels. It is not just about the quantity of food but the quality. Foods high in refined sugars and unhealthy fats may provide a quick energy boost, but they often lead to crashes that leave you feeling worse than before. On the contrary, a diet emphasizing complex carbohydrates, lean proteins, healthy fats, and plenty of fruits and vegetables supports steady energy throughout the day and promotes overall health and well-being.

1.2 Sustainable Nutrition for a Busy Lifestyle

In the hustle and bustle of modern life, many people find it challenging to maintain a nutritious diet. The demands of work, family, and social obligations can make it seem impossible to eat healthily. However, with the right strategies, it is possible to nourish your body properly without spending hours in the kitchen or resorting to fast food.

One of the key strategies for maintaining a healthy diet despite a busy schedule is planning. Meal planning allows you to organize your meals in advance, ensuring that you have nutritious options available when time is tight. This can help prevent the temptation to grab unhealthy, convenient foods that provide little nutritional value. By dedicating a small amount of time each week to plan your meals, you can save time and stress during the week, knowing that you have healthy meals ready to go.

Batch cooking is another effective strategy. By preparing large quantities of food at once, you can have ready-made meals or components of meals that can be quickly assembled during the week. For example, cooking a large pot of quinoa or roasting a tray of vegetables on the weekend can provide the base for several meals. These components can be mixed and matched with other ingredients to create a variety of dishes, reducing the need for daily cooking.

Incorporating quick and easy recipes into your routine is also essential. Many healthy meals can be prepared in under 30 minutes with minimal ingredients. Focusing on recipes that require only a few steps and use pantry staples can make healthy eating more accessible. For instance, a simple stir-fry with vegetables, lean protein, and whole grains can be prepared quickly and provides a balanced, nutritious meal.

Another approach to sustainable nutrition is to simplify your meals. Eating well does not have to be complicated or time-consuming. Some of the healthiest meals are also the simplest—think of a salad with mixed greens, grilled chicken, avocado, and a drizzle of olive oil, or a bowl of oatmeal topped with fresh berries and nuts. These meals require minimal preparation yet are packed with nutrients that support energy and well-being.

Mindful eating is another practice that can help maintain a healthy diet. In our busy lives, it is easy to eat on the go or while distracted, leading to overeating or poor food choices. Taking the time to eat slowly and savor each bite can help you tune in to your body's hunger and fullness cues, making it easier to eat the right amount of food and choose healthier options.

For those with particularly hectic schedules, incorporating snacks that provide sustained energy is crucial. Having a stash of healthy snacks, such as nuts, fruit, or yogurt, can help keep your energy levels stable throughout the day and prevent energy dips between meals. These snacks should be easy to carry and require little to no preparation, making them ideal for busy days.

Another important aspect of sustainable nutrition is making healthier choices when eating out. While it is generally healthier to cook at home, dining out is a reality for many people. Learning to navigate restaurant menus and make healthier choices can help you maintain a nutritious diet even when eating out. Opt for grilled rather than fried foods, choose dishes that include plenty of vegetables, and watch portion sizes to avoid overeating.

1.3 How to Use This Book

This cookbook is designed not just as a collection of recipes but as a comprehensive guide to transforming your diet and lifestyle. Whether you are a novice in the kitchen or an experienced home cook, this book offers valuable resources to help you incorporate nutritious meals into your daily routine, all while keeping your energy levels high and your life stress-free.

The book is structured to be user-friendly and adaptable to your needs. Each chapter focuses on a specific aspect of daily nutrition, from energizing breakfasts to satisfying dinners, and includes a variety of recipes that are both easy to prepare and nutritionally balanced. In addition to the recipes, you'll find practical advice on meal planning, tips for batch cooking, and strategies for maintaining a healthy diet despite a busy schedule.

One of the unique features of this book is the 28-day meal plan, which is designed to help you kickstart your wellness journey. The meal plan provides a structured yet flexible approach to eating, ensuring that you receive a balanced intake of nutrients while exploring a wide range of delicious recipes. Here's how you can make the most of the meal plan and the recipes in this book:

- Start with the Meal Plan: The 28-day meal plan is an excellent starting point if you're looking to overhaul your diet or simply need guidance on what to eat. It's structured to provide variety, so you won't get bored with your meals, and it's balanced to ensure you get all the necessary nutrients. Follow the plan as closely as possible for the best results, but feel free to swap out recipes based on your preferences or dietary needs.

- Adapt to Your Lifestyle: While the meal plan offers a structured approach, it's important to adapt it to your lifestyle. If you have a particularly busy week, you might focus more on the quick and easy recipes. If you're cooking for a family, you can scale the recipes to serve more people or adjust the ingredients to cater to everyone's tastes. The book includes recipes that are easy to modify, making it suitable for different lifestyles and dietary requirements.

- Use the Recipes Independently: Even if you're not following the meal plan, the recipes can still serve as valuable resources. Each recipe is designed to be nutritionally balanced and energy-boosting, making them perfect for individual meals. Whether you need a quick breakfast, a packed lunch, or a comforting dinner, you can pick and choose recipes based on what you need that day.

- Focus on Nutritional Information: Each recipe includes nutritional information to help you understand what you're eating and how it fits into your overall diet. Pay attention to the calorie count, macronutrient breakdown (carbohydrates, proteins, fats), and any specific vitamins or minerals highlighted. This information can be particularly useful if you have specific dietary goals, such as weight loss, muscle gain, or managing a health condition.

- Incorporate the Tips and Advice: Scattered throughout the book, you'll find tips and advice that can enhance your cooking and eating experience. These include suggestions for ingredient substitutions, tips for saving time in the kitchen, and advice on how to store and reheat leftovers. These tips are designed to make healthy eating more accessible and sustainable, no matter how busy your schedule is.

- Engage with the Visuals: For some recipes, images are included to give you a visual reference for how the final dish should look. These images can be especially helpful if you're trying a recipe for the first time. Visuals can also inspire you to experiment with presentation and make your meals more appealing.

- Customize According to Dietary Preferences: This book acknowledges that dietary preferences and needs vary greatly from person to person. If you follow a vegetarian, vegan, gluten-free, or keto diet, there are plenty of recipes that cater specifically to these preferences. Additionally, many recipes include suggestions for how to modify them to suit different dietary needs.

1.4 Balancing Macro and Micronutrients

Achieving a balanced diet is key to maintaining energy levels and overall health, and this balance hinges on getting the right mix of macronutrients (carbohydrates, proteins, and fats) and micronutrients (vitamins and minerals). Each nutrient plays a distinct role in the body, and understanding how to combine them effectively in your meals will help you get the most out of your diet.

Macronutrients: The Building Blocks of Energy

- Carbohydrates: Carbohydrates are often seen as the body's primary energy source because they break down into glucose, which fuels our cells. However, not all carbs are equal. This book emphasizes the importance of choosing complex carbohydrates, which are digested slowly and provide a steady release of energy. Foods like whole grains, vegetables, and legumes fall into this category. In contrast, simple carbohydrates, found in sugary snacks and refined grains, should be limited as they can lead to energy spikes followed by crashes.

  In the recipes included in this book, you'll find that carbohydrates are balanced to avoid overwhelming your system with sugar. Whole grains such as brown rice, quinoa, and oats are frequently used, as are starchy vegetables like sweet potatoes and legumes. These ingredients ensure that your energy levels remain consistent throughout the day.

- Proteins: Proteins are essential for building and repairing tissues, including muscles, and they also play a role in enzyme and hormone production. While proteins are not the body's first choice for energy, they are vital for long-term health and maintaining muscle mass. Additionally, proteins have a high satiety factor, meaning they help you feel full for longer, which can prevent overeating.

The recipes in this book feature a variety of protein sources, from lean meats like chicken and turkey to plant-based options such as tofu, tempeh, and legumes. The balance of plant-based and animal proteins ensures that you can tailor your diet to your preferences and nutritional needs.

- Fats: Fats are often misunderstood, but they are a crucial part of a healthy diet. Fats provide more energy per gram than carbohydrates or proteins and are essential for absorbing fat-soluble vitamins (A, D, E, and K). Healthy fats, such as those found in avocados, nuts, seeds, and olive oil, support brain function, reduce inflammation, and provide long-lasting energy.

The recipes in this book prioritize healthy fats over unhealthy, trans fats and saturated fats. Ingredients like olive oil, nuts, seeds, and fatty fish are common, ensuring that you get the necessary fats to support both energy levels and overall health.

Micronutrients: The Silent Supporters

- Vitamins: Vitamins are organic compounds that the body needs in small quantities for a variety of functions, including energy production, immune function, and bone health. For example, B vitamins are crucial in converting food into usable energy, while vitamin C is important for immune health and acts as an antioxidant.

This book includes a variety of fruits and vegetables rich in essential vitamins. Citrus fruits, berries, leafy greens, and bell peppers are commonly used, ensuring that your diet is rich in vitamins that support overall health.

- Minerals: Minerals such as calcium, magnesium, potassium, and iron play critical roles in maintaining energy, supporting muscle function, and building strong bones. Iron, for example, is essential for oxygen transport in the blood, and a deficiency can lead to fatigue.

The recipes emphasize mineral-rich foods like leafy greens, nuts, seeds, legumes, and whole grains. These ingredients help ensure that you're getting enough of these critical nutrients to support your energy and well-being.

Achieving Balance in Every Meal

Balancing macronutrients and micronutrients in your meals can seem daunting, but the recipes in this book are designed to make it simple. Each recipe is crafted to include a balance of carbohydrates, proteins, and fats, along with a variety of fruits and vegetables that provide essential vitamins and minerals. For example, a typical meal might include a protein source like grilled chicken, a complex carbohydrate like quinoa, and a mix of vegetables, all drizzled with a healthy fat like olive oil. This combination not only ensures a balanced intake of nutrients but also keeps you full and energized for hours.

To help you create well-balanced meals, this book includes a guide to portion sizes and food combinations that optimize nutrient intake. For example, pairing vitamin C-rich foods with iron-rich plant foods can enhance iron absorption, a tip that is particularly useful for those following a vegetarian diet.

In addition to balancing nutrients within each meal, it's important to consider balance throughout the day. The recipes are categorized into meals and snacks that fit together to form a comprehensive daily intake of nutrients. This approach helps prevent nutrient deficiencies and supports sustained energy levels from morning to night.

The Role of Supplements

While this book emphasizes getting nutrients from whole foods, there may be cases where supplements are necessary, particularly if you have specific dietary restrictions or health conditions. However, supplements should complement a balanced diet, not replace it. The focus should always be on consuming a variety of nutrient-dense foods that naturally provide the vitamins and minerals your body needs.

In conclusion, balancing macro and micronutrients is essential for maintaining energy levels, supporting overall health, and optimizing your diet. By following the recipes and guidelines in this book, you can create meals that are not only delicious but also nutritionally balanced, helping you to achieve your wellness goals in a sustainable and enjoyable way.

Chapter 2: Meal Planning

Meal planning is a powerful tool that can revolutionize the way you approach eating, saving you time, money, and stress. In this chapter, we will delve into the various benefits of meal planning, provide a step-by-step guide to creating your own weekly meal plan, and introduce the 28-day meal plan included in this book. Whether you're new to meal planning or looking to refine your approach, this chapter will equip you with the knowledge and strategies needed to make meal planning a seamless part of your routine.

2.1 Benefits of Meal Planning

Meal planning is often lauded as a key strategy for maintaining a healthy diet, but its benefits extend far beyond just nutrition. When done correctly, meal planning can streamline your life in several meaningful ways, helping you save time, reduce stress, cut down on food waste, and even lower your grocery bills.

Saving Time and Reducing Stress

One of the most immediate benefits of meal planning is the significant amount of time it can save. In our busy lives, the daily question of "What's for dinner?" can be a source of stress, particularly when time is short and hunger levels are high. By planning your meals in advance, you eliminate the need for daily decision-making around food. Instead, you can simply follow the plan you've set, knowing that you have all the ingredients on hand and that your meals are nutritionally balanced.

Meal planning also reduces the time spent on grocery shopping. With a detailed meal plan, you can create a precise shopping list, ensuring that you buy only what you need for the week. This focused approach to shopping not only saves time but also reduces the likelihood of impulse purchases, which are often less healthy and more expensive.

Additionally, having a meal plan means that you can batch cook and prepare ingredients ahead of time, further saving time during the week. For example, if your plan includes several recipes that use quinoa, you can cook a large batch at the beginning of the week and use it in multiple dishes. This minimizes the amount of daily cooking required and allows you to quickly assemble meals.

Reducing Food Waste

Food waste is a significant issue both environmentally and economically.

When food is wasted, the resources used to produce, transport, and store that food are also wasted. Meal planning helps to reduce food waste by ensuring that you only buy what you need and use everything you purchase.

By planning your meals around ingredients you already have on hand, you can use up perishable items before they spoil. For instance, if you have a surplus of vegetables, you can plan meals that incorporate those ingredients to avoid throwing them away. Similarly, by planning meals that share ingredients, you can make sure that items like fresh herbs or specialty ingredients don't go to waste.

This thoughtful approach to meal planning not only reduces waste but also encourages creativity in the kitchen. You may find yourself experimenting with new recipes or combinations of ingredients that you wouldn't have considered otherwise, all while making the most of what you have.

Saving Money

Meal planning is also a powerful tool for saving money. When you plan your meals and create a shopping list, you can avoid the financial pitfalls of last-minute takeout orders or frequent trips to the grocery store. By sticking to your plan, you can limit impulse buys and focus on purchasing only the items you need.

Moreover, meal planning allows you to take advantage of sales and bulk purchases. For example, if you know you'll be using chicken in several meals over the week, you can buy it in bulk, which is often cheaper than buying smaller portions multiple times. Planning meals around seasonal produce can also help reduce costs, as fruits and vegetables that are in season are typically less expensive and more flavorful.

In addition to saving money on groceries, meal planning can help reduce the costs associated with food waste. By using up all the ingredients you buy, you maximize the value of your grocery purchases. Over time, these savings can add up, making a noticeable difference in your household budget.

Improving Nutritional Quality

Another key benefit of meal planning is that it allows you to take control of your diet, ensuring that your meals are balanced and aligned with your nutritional goals. When you plan your meals in advance, you can consciously include a variety of foods that provide the necessary macronutrients (carbohydrates, proteins, and fats) and micronutrients (vitamins and minerals).

Meal planning also helps prevent the reliance on convenience foods, which are often high in unhealthy fats, sugars, and sodium. Instead, you can focus on preparing whole, nutrient-dense meals that support your energy levels and overall health. By including a mix of vegetables, lean proteins, whole grains, and healthy fats in your plan, you can ensure that your diet is both satisfying and nourishing.

Additionally, if you have specific dietary needs or health goals—such as weight loss, managing a chronic condition, or following a plant-based diet—meal planning allows you to tailor your meals accordingly. You can monitor portion sizes, control ingredients, and make adjustments based on your progress, all of which contribute to better long-term health outcomes.

Enhancing Variety and Enjoyment

Finally, meal planning can enhance the variety and enjoyment of your meals. Without a plan, it's easy to fall into the habit of eating the same few dishes repeatedly, which can lead to boredom and diminish the overall eating experience. With meal planning, you can consciously introduce a wider range of foods and flavors into your diet.

This book includes a diverse array of recipes that cater to different tastes, dietary preferences, and seasonal ingredients. By incorporating these recipes into your meal plan, you can ensure that your meals are both exciting and nutritious. Trying new recipes and ingredients can also expand your culinary skills and introduce you to new favorite dishes.

2.2 How to Create a Weekly Meal Plan

Creating a weekly meal plan may seem daunting at first, but with a clear strategy and a bit of practice, it can become a seamless part of your routine. The key is to start with a plan that is realistic and adaptable to your lifestyle, gradually refining your approach as you become more comfortable with the process. Here's a step-by-step guide to help you create an effective weekly meal plan:

Step 1: Assess Your Week

The first step in creating a meal plan is to assess your upcoming week. Take into account your work schedule, social commitments, and any other activities that might affect your meal times. If you know you'll have a particularly busy day, you might plan a quick and easy meal for that evening. Conversely, if you have more free time on a certain day, you could plan a more elaborate meal or use that time for batch cooking.

It's also important to consider who you'll be cooking for. If you're cooking for a family, you'll need to plan meals that cater to everyone's preferences and dietary needs. If you're cooking just for yourself, you might plan to make larger portions that can be used as leftovers or frozen for later in the week.

Step 2: Set Your Meal Planning Goals

Next, define your goals for the week. Are you aiming to eat more vegetables? Do you want to try new recipes? Are you focusing on portion control or managing your caloric intake? Setting specific goals can help guide your meal choices and ensure that your plan aligns with your health objectives.

Your goals might also include non-nutritional factors, such as reducing food waste, saving money, or incorporating more seasonal ingredients. Whatever your goals, keep them in mind as you move forward with the planning process.

Step 3: Choose Your Recipes

With your week and goals in mind, it's time to choose your recipes. Start by browsing through the recipes in this book, focusing on those that align with your goals and the amount of time you have available. You might choose a mix of recipes that are quick and easy, along with a few that are more time-intensive for when you have extra time to cook.

As you select your recipes, consider how they fit together. For example, if you're making a recipe that requires a specific ingredient like fresh herbs or a particular spice, look for other recipes that use the same ingredient to avoid waste. Similarly, if you're batch cooking, choose recipes that can be easily reheated or repurposed into different meals.

It's also helpful to plan for variety. Include different types of proteins (e.g., chicken, tofu, beans), a range of vegetables, and a mix of flavors to keep your meals interesting. You might also plan a few themed meals, such as a "Meatless Monday" or a "Taco Tuesday," to add some fun and structure to your week.

Step 4: Make a Shopping List

Once you've chosen your recipes, the next step is to make a shopping list. Write down all the ingredients you'll need for the week, taking care to check your pantry and refrigerator for items you already have. Organize your list by category (e.g., produce, dairy, grains) to make your shopping trip more efficient.

As you make your list, consider how much of each ingredient you'll need, especially for perishable items. If you're unsure about quantities, it's better to buy a little less and plan to supplement with pantry staples if needed. This approach helps minimize waste and ensures that you use up what you buy.

Step 5: Plan for Leftovers and Flexibility

A key aspect of successful meal planning is allowing for flexibility. Life can be unpredictable, and there may be times when you need to adjust your plan. For this reason, it's a good idea to plan for leftovers that can be used for lunches or quick dinners later in the week.

You might also include a few "backup" meals—simple dishes

that you can throw together quickly if your plans change. For example, having the ingredients for a basic pasta dish or a stir-fry can be a lifesaver on nights when you're too tired to cook the meal you originally planned.

Step 6: Prep in Advance

With your plan in place and your ingredients purchased, the final step is to prep as much as possible in advance. This could mean washing and chopping vegetables, cooking grains, or marinating proteins. Preparing these components ahead of time makes it easier to assemble meals during the week, especially on busy days.

Batch cooking is another effective strategy. If you're making a dish like soup, stew, or casserole, consider doubling the recipe and freezing half for later. This not only saves time but also ensures you have healthy, homemade meals ready to go when needed.

Step 7: Stick to the Plan, but Stay Flexible

As the week unfolds, do your best to stick to your meal plan, but remember that flexibility is key. If something unexpected comes up, don't stress about deviating from the plan. Simply adjust as needed and use the meals or ingredients you had planned later in the week or the following week.

By following these steps, meal planning can become a manageable and even enjoyable part of your routine. With practice, you'll find that it helps simplify your life, reduce stress, and make healthy eating more achievable.

2.3 The 28-Day Meal Plan

To help you jumpstart your journey to better health, this book includes a comprehensive 28-day meal plan. This plan is designed to guide you through a month of nutritious eating, providing structure and variety while introducing you to the recipes and strategies outlined in this book.

Whether you're looking to reset your eating habits, lose weight, or simply try new foods, the 28-day meal plan offers a balanced and flexible approach to achieving your goals.

Overview of the Plan

The 28-day meal plan is divided into four weeks, each with its own set of recipes and meal suggestions. Each week is carefully curated to ensure that you receive a balanced intake of nutrients, with a focus on whole, minimally processed foods. The plan includes breakfast, lunch, dinner, and snacks, with options that cater to different dietary preferences and needs.

Each week, you'll find a mix of familiar recipes and new dishes to keep your meals interesting and enjoyable. The plan also incorporates seasonal ingredients, making it easier to find fresh produce and take advantage of the flavors of the season.

How to Follow the Plan

The 28-day meal plan is designed to be flexible and adaptable. While it provides a structured approach to eating, it's not meant to be rigid or restrictive. Here's how you can make the most of the plan:

- Follow It as Closely as Possible: For the best results, try to follow the meal plan as closely as you can. This will help you stay on track with your nutritional goals and ensure that you're getting a balanced diet. However, don't worry if you need to make adjustments—life happens, and the plan is meant to fit into your lifestyle, not the other way around.

- Customize the Plan to Your Needs: The meal plan is designed to be a starting point. Feel free to modify the recipes or swap out meals based on your preferences, dietary restrictions, or what you have on hand. For example, if you're vegetarian, you can replace meat-based recipes with plant-based alternatives, many of which are included in the plan.

- Incorporate Leftovers: The plan includes suggestions for using leftovers to minimize waste and save time. For example, if a recipe makes more than you need for one meal, you can use the leftovers for lunch the next day or freeze them for later in the week.

- Adjust Portion Sizes: Depending on your individual needs and goals, you may need to adjust the portion sizes in the meal plan. If you're trying to lose weight, you might reduce portion sizes slightly, while those looking to maintain or gain weight might increase portions.

- Use the Plan as Inspiration: Even if you don't follow the plan exactly, it can serve as inspiration for your meals. You might choose to follow the plan for a few days each week, or you could mix and match recipes from different weeks to create your own customized plan.

Weekly Breakdown

Here's an overview of what you can expect each week of the 28-day meal plan:

- Week 1: Getting Started
  - Focus: Introducing balanced meals and setting a foundation for the weeks ahead.
  - Highlights: Simple, easy-to-prepare recipes that help you ease into meal planning.
Includes tips for prepping ingredients and organizing your kitchen.

- Week 2: Building Momentum
  - Focus: Incorporating more variety and introducing new flavors.
  - Highlights: A mix of familiar dishes and new recipes that encourage you to expand your
palate. Includes suggestions for batch cooking and using leftovers.

- Week 3: Expanding Horizons
  - Focus: Trying new ingredients and cooking techniques.
  - Highlights: Recipes that challenge you to step out of your comfort zone and explore new
cuisines. Includes tips for staying motivated and making the plan work for you.

- Week 4: Finishing Strong
  - Focus: Solidifying healthy habits and preparing for long-term success.
  - Highlights: Recipes that focus on sustainability and simplicity. Includes advice on how to
continue meal planning after the 28 days and maintain your progress.

Conclusion

The 28-day meal plan is more than just a guide to what you should eat for a month—it's a
tool to help you build sustainable habits that support long-term health and well-being. By
following the plan, you'll learn how to create balanced, nutritious meals that fit into your
busy life, all while enjoying delicious food that nourishes your body and fuels your day.
Whether you complete the plan in its entirety or use it as a starting point for your own meal
planning, the knowledge and skills you gain will be invaluable in your journey toward better
health.

Chapter 3: Energizing Breakfasts

Breakfast is often referred to as the most important meal of the day, and for good reason. The food you consume in the morning sets the tone for your energy levels, metabolism, and overall well-being throughout the day. A well-balanced breakfast can provide the essential nutrients and sustained energy needed to power through your morning, keep your focus sharp, and prevent the mid-morning energy crashes that can derail productivity. In this chapter, we explore why starting your day with a healthy breakfast is crucial and how to create balanced morning meals that energize your body and mind.

3.1 The Importance of a Balanced Breakfast

After a night of fasting, your body wakes up in need of refueling. Breakfast, literally breaking the fast, replenishes your glucose levels, which is essential for the brain and body to function optimally. Skipping breakfast can leave you feeling sluggish, impair cognitive function, and lead to overeating later in the day. Conversely, a nutritious breakfast provides numerous benefits that contribute to better overall health and energy management.

Sustained Energy Levels

One of the primary roles of breakfast is to kickstart your metabolism and provide the energy needed to get through the morning. A balanced breakfast that includes a mix of complex carbohydrates, protein, and healthy fats can help stabilize blood sugar levels, preventing the spikes and crashes that often result from eating sugary or highly processed foods. Complex carbohydrates, such as those found in whole grains, fruits, and vegetables, are digested more slowly, providing a steady release of glucose into the bloodstream. This slow digestion helps maintain energy levels over several hours, reducing the likelihood of fatigue or the need for a mid-morning snack.

Proteins play a crucial role in maintaining satiety and supporting muscle function. Including a source of protein in your breakfast, such as eggs, yogurt, or plant-based options like tofu or nuts, helps to keep you feeling full longer, which can prevent overeating at subsequent meals. Protein also contributes to the maintenance and repair of tissues, including muscles, which is important for overall physical health and stamina.

Healthy fats, found in foods like avocados, nuts, seeds, and olive oil, are another important component of a balanced breakfast. Fats are energy-dense, providing a sustained source of fuel for the body. They also aid in the absorption of fat-soluble vitamins (A, D, E, and K), which are vital for various bodily functions, including immune support and skin health. Including healthy fats in your breakfast helps to create a meal that is not only satisfying but also nutritionally complete.

Improved Cognitive Function and Mood

Your brain relies heavily on glucose for energy, and without adequate fuel, cognitive functions such as concentration, memory, and problem-solving can suffer. A balanced breakfast that includes carbohydrates, especially from whole grains or fruits, provides the glucose your brain needs to operate at its best. Studies have shown that individuals who eat breakfast tend to have better memory, attention, and overall cognitive performance compared to those who skip the morning meal.

Moreover, the nutrients provided by a balanced breakfast contribute to better mood regulation. For instance, complex carbohydrates increase the production of serotonin, a neurotransmitter that promotes feelings of well-being and happiness. Proteins provide amino acids like tryptophan, which are precursors to serotonin, further supporting mood stability. Healthy fats contribute to the structure and function of brain cells, supporting overall mental health.

Skipping breakfast or eating a meal high in simple sugars can lead to irritability, mood swings, and difficulty concentrating as blood sugar levels fluctuate. On the other hand, a well-balanced breakfast helps to maintain stable blood sugar levels, which supports a calm and focused mindset throughout the morning.

Weight Management and Metabolic Health

There is a common misconception that skipping breakfast can aid in weight loss, but the opposite is often true. Eating a balanced breakfast can actually support weight management by preventing overeating later in the day. When you skip breakfast, your body remains in a fasting state, which can lead to increased hunger and cravings, particularly for high-calorie, sugary foods. This can result in consuming more calories overall, often in the form of snacks or larger portions at lunch and dinner.

Starting your day with a nutritious breakfast helps to kickstart your metabolism, enabling your body to burn calories more efficiently throughout the day. Additionally, the satiety provided by a balanced breakfast reduces the likelihood of snacking on unhealthy foods between meals, making it easier to maintain a healthy weight.

Breakfast also plays a role in regulating insulin levels. Regularly eating a balanced breakfast can help improve insulin sensitivity, which is important for preventing type 2 diabetes and other metabolic disorders. A meal that includes whole grains, lean proteins, and healthy fats helps to moderate blood sugar levels, reducing the risk of insulin spikes that can lead to insulin resistance over time.

Long-Term Health Benefits

The benefits of a balanced breakfast extend beyond daily energy and focus. Consistently eating a nutritious morning meal is associated with long-term health benefits, including a reduced risk of chronic diseases such as heart disease, type 2 diabetes, and obesity. Whole grains, fruits, and vegetables consumed at breakfast contribute to a higher intake of fiber, vitamins, and minerals, which are essential for maintaining overall health and preventing disease.

For example, fiber-rich foods like oatmeal or whole grain bread support digestive health by promoting regular bowel movements and preventing constipation. Fiber also helps to lower cholesterol levels and regulate blood sugar, reducing the risk of heart disease and diabetes.

Including fruits and vegetables in your breakfast increases your intake of antioxidants, which protect your cells from damage caused by free radicals. This can help prevent inflammation and reduce the risk of chronic diseases.

3.2 Quick Breakfast Recipes

Recipe List:

Green Detox Smoothie

Ingredients:
- 1 cup spinach leaves
- 1/2 cucumber, chopped
- 1 small green apple, cored and chopped
- 1/2 lemon, juiced
- 1-inch piece of ginger, peeled
- 1 tablespoon chia seeds
- 1 cup coconut water or water
- Ice cubes (optional)

Instructions:
1. Place the spinach, cucumber, green apple, lemon juice, and ginger in a blender.
2. Add the chia seeds and coconut water.
3. Blend until smooth and creamy.
4. Add ice cubes for a colder smoothie if desired.
5. Pour into a glass and enjoy immediately.

Oatmeal with Berries

Ingredients:
- 1/2 cup rolled oats
- 1 cup water or milk
- 1/2 teaspoon cinnamon
- 1/2 cup mixed berries (e.g., blueberries, raspberries, strawberries)
- 1 tablespoon honey or maple syrup (optional)
- 1 tablespoon nuts or seeds (optional)

Instructions:
1. In a small pot, bring the water or milk to a boil.
2. Add the oats and cinnamon, reduce heat, and simmer for 5 minutes, stirring occasionally.
3. Remove from heat and top with mixed berries, honey, and nuts or seeds if using.
4. Serve warm.

Buckwheat Protein Pancakes

Ingredients:
- 1/2 cup buckwheat flour
- 1 scoop protein powder (vanilla or unflavored)
- 1/2 teaspoon baking powder
- 1 egg
- 1/2 cup milk (dairy or plant-based)
- 1 teaspoon vanilla extract
- 1 tablespoon coconut oil (for cooking)

Instructions:
1. In a bowl, mix the buckwheat flour, protein powder, and baking powder.
2. Whisk in the egg, milk, and vanilla until smooth.
3. Heat coconut oil in a skillet over medium heat.
4. Pour small amounts of batter into the skillet to form pancakes.
5. Cook for 2-3 minutes on each side or until golden brown.
6. Serve with your favorite toppings like fresh fruit, yogurt, or honey.

Wholegrain Avocado and Poached Egg Toast

Ingredients:
- 2 slices wholegrain bread
- 1 ripe avocado
- 2 eggs
- 1 tablespoon vinegar
- Salt and pepper, to taste
- Red pepper flakes (optional)

Instructions:
1. Toast the wholegrain bread until golden brown.
2. Mash the avocado in a bowl and season with salt and pepper.
3. Spread the avocado evenly over the toasted bread slices.
4. In a pot, bring water and vinegar to a simmer. Crack eggs into the water and poach for 3-4 minutes.
5. Remove eggs with a slotted spoon and place them on the avocado toast.
6. Sprinkle with red pepper flakes if desired, and serve immediately.

Chia Pudding with Coconut Milk and Mango

Ingredients:
- 1/4 cup chia seeds
- 1 cup coconut milk
- 1 tablespoon honey or maple syrup
- 1 ripe mango, peeled and diced

Instructions:
1. In a bowl, mix chia seeds, coconut milk, and honey.

2. Stir well to combine and let sit for 10 minutes. Stir again to prevent clumping.
3. Refrigerate for at least 2 hours or overnight until thickened.
4. Top with diced mango before serving.

Egg White Frittata with Spinach and Cherry Tomatoes

Ingredients:
- 4 egg whites
- 1 cup fresh spinach
- 1/2 cup cherry tomatoes, halved
- 1/4 cup onion, finely chopped
- Salt and pepper, to taste
- 1 teaspoon olive oil

Instructions:
1. Preheat the oven to 350°F (175°C).
2. In an oven-safe skillet, heat olive oil over medium heat. Sauté the onions until soft.
3. Add spinach and cherry tomatoes, cooking until spinach wilts.
4. Pour in egg whites, season with salt and pepper, and cook for 2 minutes without stirring.
5. Transfer the skillet to the oven and bake for 10-12 minutes until the frittata is set.
6. Slice and serve warm.

Crunchy Granola with Nuts and Honey

Ingredients:
- 2 cups rolled oats
- 1/2 cup mixed nuts (almonds, walnuts, pecans), chopped
- 1/4 cup sunflower seeds
- 1/4 cup honey

- 2 tablespoons coconut oil, melted
- 1 teaspoon vanilla extract
- 1/2 teaspoon cinnamon
- Pinch of salt

Instructions:
1. Preheat the oven to 300°F (150°C) and line a baking sheet with parchment paper.
2. In a large bowl, mix oats, nuts, seeds, cinnamon, and salt.
3. Add honey, melted coconut oil, and vanilla extract; stir until evenly coated.
4. Spread the mixture onto the baking sheet in an even layer.
5. Bake for 25-30 minutes, stirring halfway, until golden and crunchy.
6. Let it cool completely before storing in an airtight container.

Apple Cinnamon Overnight Oats

Ingredients:
- 1/2 cup rolled oats
- 1/2 cup milk (dairy or plant-based)
- 1/4 cup unsweetened applesauce
- 1/2 teaspoon cinnamon
- 1 tablespoon chia seeds
- 1/4 apple, diced
- Honey or maple syrup (optional)

Instructions:
1. In a jar or bowl, combine oats, milk, applesauce, cinnamon, and chia seeds.
2. Stir well, then top with diced apple.
3. Cover and refrigerate overnight.
4. In the morning, stir and add honey or syrup if desired.

Wholegrain Banana Nut Muffins

Ingredients:
- 1 1/2 cups wholegrain flour
- 1 teaspoon baking soda
- 1/2 teaspoon salt
- 1/2 teaspoon cinnamon
- 3 ripe bananas, mashed
- 1/3 cup honey or maple syrup
- 1/4 cup coconut oil, melted
- 1 egg

- 1 teaspoon vanilla extract
- 1/2 cup chopped walnuts

Instructions:
1. Preheat the oven to 350°F (175°C) and line a muffin tin with paper liners.
2. In a bowl, mix flour, baking soda, salt, and cinnamon.
3. In another bowl, combine mashed bananas, honey, coconut oil, egg, and vanilla.
4. Gradually add dry ingredients to the wet ingredients, stirring until just combined.
5. Fold in the chopped walnuts.
6. Pour the batter into the muffin tin and bake for 20-25 minutes, or until a toothpick comes out clean.

Tropical Fruit Smoothie Bowl

Ingredients:
- 1/2 cup frozen mango chunks
- 1/2 cup frozen pineapple chunks
- 1/2 banana
- 1/2 cup coconut milk or almond milk
- 1 tablespoon chia seeds
- Toppings: sliced kiwi, coconut flakes, granola, fresh berries

Instructions:
1. In a blender, combine frozen mango, pineapple, banana, and coconut milk.
2. Blend until smooth and creamy.
3. Pour the smoothie into a bowl.
4. Top with sliced kiwi, coconut flakes, granola, and fresh berries.
5. Serve immediately and enjoy.

Almond Butter Banana Toast

Ingredients:
- 2 slices wholegrain bread
- 2 tablespoons almond butter
- 1 banana, sliced
- 1 teaspoon honey (optional)
- 1/2 teaspoon cinnamon

Instructions:
1. Toast the wholegrain bread until golden brown.
2. Spread almond butter evenly over each slice.
3. Arrange banana slices on top of the almond butter.
4. Drizzle with honey if desired, and sprinkle with cinnamon.
5. Serve immediately for a quick and healthy breakfast.

Greek Yogurt Parfait with Granola and Berries

Ingredients:
- 1 cup Greek yogurt
- 1/4 cup granola
- 1/2 cup mixed berries (blueberries, strawberries, raspberries)
- 1 tablespoon honey or maple syrup (optional)

Instructions:
1. In a glass or bowl, layer half of the Greek yogurt at the bottom.
2. Add a layer of granola and then a layer of mixed berries.
3. Repeat the layers with the remaining yogurt, granola, and berries.
4. Drizzle with honey or maple syrup if desired.
5. Serve immediately or refrigerate for later.

3.3 Breakfast Meal Prep

In the rush of morning routines, it can be challenging to find time to prepare a nutritious breakfast. However, with a bit of planning and preparation, you can ensure that you start your day with a healthy, energizing meal without spending too much time in the kitchen. Breakfast meal prep is the solution to this common dilemma, allowing you to prepare your morning meals in advance so that they're ready to go when you need them. This section will explore various tips and strategies for making breakfast meal prep a seamless part of your routine, ensuring that you have quick, delicious, and nutritious options ready every morning.

Plan Your Week

The first step in breakfast meal prep is planning your week. Take some time over the weekend or at the beginning of your week to decide what you want to eat for breakfast over the next few days. Consider your schedule and how much time you'll have in the mornings. If you know certain days will be busier, focus on grab-and-go options like smoothies or overnight oats. For mornings when you have a bit more time, you might prep ingredients for a quick-cook meal like a frittata or breakfast burrito.

Having a plan ensures that you can shop for the necessary ingredients and allocate time for meal prep. It also prevents the stress of deciding what to eat at the last minute, which often leads to less healthy choices.

Batch Cooking

Batch cooking is a highly effective strategy for breakfast meal prep. By preparing large quantities of food at once, you can have several days' worth of breakfasts ready to go. Foods that store well and reheat easily are ideal for batch cooking.

For example, you can bake a large batch of muffins or granola at the start of the week. Muffins made with whole grains, fruits, and nuts are not only filling but also easy to store. You can refrigerate them for up to a week or freeze them for longer storage. Granola is another excellent option—prepare a big batch and store it in an airtight container to enjoy with yogurt or milk throughout the week.

Egg-based dishes like frittatas or breakfast casseroles are also great for batch cooking. Prepare a large frittata filled with vegetables and protein, then slice it into portions that can be quickly reheated in the morning. These dishes typically keep well in the refrigerator for several days and can be paired with wholegrain toast or a side of fruit for a complete breakfast.

Overnight Preparations

Some breakfasts can be prepared the night before, making your mornings even easier. Overnight oats are a popular and versatile option. Combine rolled oats with milk or a plant-based alternative, add your favorite mix-ins like chia seeds, nuts, or fruit, and let it sit in the refrigerator overnight. In the morning, your oats will be ready to eat—no cooking required. You can also warm them up if you prefer a hot breakfast.

Chia pudding is another overnight option. Mix chia seeds with coconut milk or almond milk and a bit of sweetener, then refrigerate overnight. In the morning, top it with fresh fruit, nuts, or granola for a quick, nutrient-packed breakfast.

For those who enjoy smoothies, consider prepping smoothie packs in advance. Measure out your fruits, vegetables, and other ingredients like protein powder or seeds, and store them in freezer-safe bags. In the morning, just add your liquid base, like water, milk, or juice, and blend. This not only saves time but also ensures you always have the ingredients for a healthy smoothie on hand.

Portion Control and Storage

When prepping breakfast in advance, it's important to consider portion control. Pre-portioning your meals ensures that you're eating the right amount and makes it easier to grab a meal and go. For example, if you've made a batch of breakfast burritos or sandwiches, wrap them individually in foil or parchment paper and store them in the refrigerator or freezer. This way, you can easily take one out in the morning, heat it, and be on your way.

Proper storage is also key to maintaining the freshness and quality of your prepped breakfasts. Invest in high-quality, airtight containers that can keep your food fresh for several days. For items like overnight oats or chia pudding, mason jars are a popular option because they are easy to store and carry.

If you're freezing items like muffins, pancakes, or breakfast sandwiches, wrap them tightly to prevent freezer burn and label them with the date so you can keep track of how long they've been stored. Most breakfast items will keep well in the freezer for up to three months.

Mix and Match Components

Another effective strategy for breakfast meal prep is to prepare various components that can be mixed and matched throughout the week. For example, you might prepare a large batch of roasted vegetables, cook some quinoa or whole grains, and make a few hard-boiled eggs. These components can be stored separately in the refrigerator and combined in different ways to create a variety of breakfasts.

One morning, you might have a grain bowl with quinoa, roasted veggies, and a poached egg. The next day, you could make a breakfast wrap using the same ingredients, adding avocado and a bit of salsa. This approach keeps your breakfasts interesting and ensures you're not eating the same thing every day.

Quick and Easy Options

Not every breakfast needs to be fully prepped in advance—sometimes, just having a few key ingredients ready to go can make all the difference. For example, keeping a supply of wholegrain bread, nut butter, and fresh fruit on hand means you can quickly make a healthy toast in the morning. Similarly, having a few pre-cooked eggs in the refrigerator allows you to whip up a quick egg and veggie scramble or add protein to a breakfast salad.

Yogurt parfaits are another quick option. Keep granola and fresh or frozen berries on hand so you can assemble a parfait in minutes. Layer Greek yogurt with granola and berries in a jar or bowl, and you have a nutritious breakfast that's ready to eat immediately.

Keep It Simple

Finally, one of the most important tips for breakfast meal prep is to keep it simple. You don't need to prepare elaborate meals every morning—focus on recipes that are easy to make, store well, and provide the nutrition you need. Simple dishes like oatmeal, smoothies, and egg-based breakfasts can be varied in countless ways, so you never get bored.

In conclusion, breakfast meal prep is a game-changer for busy mornings. By planning ahead, batch cooking, and preparing ingredients in advance, you can ensure that you always have a healthy and energizing breakfast ready to go. These strategies not only save time but also help you start your day with the nutrients and energy needed to tackle whatever comes your way.

Chapter 4: Nutritious Weekday Lunches

Lunch is a crucial meal that can significantly impact your energy levels for the rest of the day. A well-balanced lunch provides the necessary nutrients to maintain focus, productivity, and overall well-being through the afternoon. However, it's easy to fall into the trap of eating quick, convenient, or heavy meals that may cause energy crashes or leave you feeling sluggish. This chapter will explore how to create balanced lunches that sustain your energy levels, ensuring you remain alert and energized throughout your day.

4.1 Lunches That Maintain Energy Levels

Maintaining steady energy levels requires a combination of macronutrients—carbohydrates, proteins, and fats—that work together to fuel your body and mind. The key is to create lunches that are not only nutritious but also satisfying and easy to prepare. Here are some tips for crafting balanced lunches that sustain energy:

Prioritize Complex Carbohydrates

Carbohydrates are your body's primary source of energy, but the type of carbohydrates you choose makes a significant difference in how your body processes and utilizes that energy. Simple carbohydrates, found in refined grains, sugary snacks, and processed foods, are quickly digested and lead to rapid spikes in blood sugar levels. These spikes are often followed by crashes, leaving you feeling tired and hungry soon after eating.

Instead, focus on incorporating complex carbohydrates into your lunches. Complex carbs, found in whole grains, legumes, and vegetables, are digested more slowly, providing a steady release of energy over several hours. They also contain more fiber, which helps you feel full and satisfied. Whole grains like quinoa, brown rice, and farro, as well as legumes such as lentils and chickpeas, are excellent choices for sustaining energy throughout the afternoon.

Include Lean Protein

Protein plays a critical role in maintaining energy levels by supporting muscle function and providing satiety. Including a source of lean protein in your lunch helps stabilize blood sugar levels and prevents mid-afternoon energy dips. Lean proteins are those that are lower in fat, such as chicken, turkey, tofu, fish, and legumes. These proteins digest at a moderate pace, providing sustained energy without the heaviness that can come from fattier cuts of meat.

A balanced lunch might include grilled chicken breast with a side of quinoa and roasted vegetables, or a chickpea salad with mixed greens and a light vinaigrette. These meals offer a good mix of protein and complex carbohydrates, helping to keep you energized and focused through the rest of the day.

Incorporate Healthy Fats

Healthy fats are essential for brain function and can help keep you feeling full and satisfied after a meal. Unlike simple carbohydrates that lead to quick energy bursts and crashes, fats provide a longer-lasting energy source. Foods rich in healthy fats include avocados, nuts, seeds, olive oil, and fatty fish like salmon. These fats are also beneficial for heart health and can help reduce inflammation in the body.

A well-balanced lunch might include a salad topped with avocado slices, a handful of nuts, or a drizzle of olive oil. Another option could be a whole grain wrap filled with salmon, mixed greens, and a light spread of hummus. These components work together to provide a balanced meal that supports both physical and cognitive function.

Focus on Fiber-Rich Foods

Fiber is another critical component of a balanced lunch that sustains energy. High-fiber foods slow down digestion, which helps regulate blood sugar levels and prolongs the feeling of fullness. This prevents the post-lunch slump that often occurs when blood sugar levels drop. Fiber-rich foods include vegetables, fruits, whole grains, and legumes.

For example, a lunch that includes a hearty vegetable soup with a whole grain roll, or a brown rice bowl topped with black beans, corn, and a variety of vegetables, provides ample fiber to support sustained energy levels. These meals are not only nutritious but also satisfying, keeping hunger at bay until your next meal.

Balance Portion Sizes

The size of your lunch also plays a role in maintaining energy levels. Overeating, even healthy foods, can lead to feelings of lethargy and sluggishness as your body works to digest a large meal. On the other hand, a lunch that is too small might leave you feeling hungry and distracted, leading to overeating later in the day.

To strike the right balance, aim for portion sizes that satisfy without overwhelming. A good rule of thumb is to fill half of your plate with vegetables, a quarter with lean protein, and a quarter with complex carbohydrates. This visual guide can help ensure that you're getting a balanced mix of nutrients in appropriate portions.

For example, a lunch that includes a grilled chicken salad with mixed greens, a small serving of whole grains like quinoa, and a side of fruit offers the right mix of nutrients in balanced portions. This approach helps maintain energy levels without causing discomfort or sluggishness.

Stay Hydrated

Hydration is often overlooked but is essential for maintaining energy levels throughout the day. Even mild dehydration can lead to fatigue, difficulty concentrating, and headaches. Be sure to drink water regularly throughout the day, especially during and after lunch.

In addition to water, you can include hydrating foods in your lunch, such as cucumbers, tomatoes, and leafy greens. These foods have high water content and can contribute to your overall hydration. Avoid sugary drinks and excessive caffeine, which can lead to energy crashes later in the day.

Prepare in Advance

One of the best ways to ensure you have a nutritious lunch that sustains energy is to prepare your meals in advance. Meal prepping on the weekend or the night before can save time and reduce the temptation to reach for less healthy, convenience foods during busy weekdays.

Consider batch cooking dishes like quinoa, grilled chicken, or roasted vegetables that can be easily combined into different lunches throughout the week. Prepping ingredients like chopped vegetables or cooked grains can also make it easier to assemble a healthy lunch in the morning or even the night before.

4.2 Quick Lunch Recipes

Recipe List:

Quinoa Salad with Grilled Vegetables

Ingredients:
- 1 cup quinoa, cooked
- 1 zucchini, sliced
- 1 red bell pepper, sliced
- 1 yellow bell pepper, sliced
- 1 small eggplant, sliced
- 2 tablespoons olive oil
- 1 tablespoon balsamic vinegar
- Salt and pepper, to taste

- 1/4 cup crumbled feta cheese (optional)
- Fresh parsley, chopped (optional)

Instructions:
1. Preheat a grill or grill pan to medium heat.
2. Toss zucchini, bell peppers, and eggplant with olive oil, salt, and pepper.
3. Grill vegetables for 5-7 minutes on each side until tender and slightly charred.
4. In a large bowl, mix cooked quinoa with grilled vegetables.
5. Drizzle with balsamic vinegar and toss to combine.
6. Top with crumbled feta cheese and fresh parsley if desired.
7. Serve warm or chilled.

Grilled Chicken Wrap with Yogurt Sauce

Ingredients:
- 2 grilled chicken breasts, sliced
- 4 wholegrain tortillas
- 1/2 cup plain Greek yogurt
- 1 tablespoon lemon juice
- 1 clove garlic, minced
- 1 cucumber, sliced
- 1 tomato, sliced
- Mixed greens
- Salt and pepper, to taste

Instructions:
1. In a small bowl, mix Greek yogurt, lemon juice, garlic, salt, and pepper to create the sauce.
2. Lay tortillas flat and spread a spoonful of yogurt sauce on each.
3. Layer with sliced chicken, cucumber, tomato, and mixed greens.
4. Roll the tortillas tightly to form wraps.
5. Serve immediately or wrap in foil for a portable lunch.

Buddha Bowl with Chickpeas and Avocado

Ingredients:
- 1 cup cooked brown rice or quinoa
- 1/2 cup cooked chickpeas
- 1/2 avocado, sliced
- 1 cup mixed greens

- 1/2 cup shredded carrots
- 1/4 cup red cabbage, sliced
- 1 tablespoon tahini
- 1 tablespoon lemon juice
- Salt and pepper, to taste
- Sesame seeds, for garnish

Instructions:
1. In a bowl, layer the cooked brown rice or quinoa as the base.
2. Add chickpeas, avocado, mixed greens, shredded carrots, and red cabbage.
3. In a small bowl, mix tahini, lemon juice, salt, and pepper to create the dressing.
4. Drizzle the dressing over the bowl.
5. Garnish with sesame seeds and serve immediately.

Spinach Salad with Smoked Salmon and Eggs

Ingredients:
- 4 cups fresh spinach leaves
- 4 ounces smoked salmon, sliced
- 2 hard-boiled eggs, sliced
- 1/2 red onion, thinly sliced
- 1/4 cup capers
- 1/2 avocado, sliced
- 2 tablespoons olive oil
- 1 tablespoon lemon juice
- Salt and pepper, to taste

Instructions:
1. In a large bowl, arrange spinach leaves as the base.
2. Top with smoked salmon, hard-boiled eggs, red onion, capers, and avocado slices.
3. Drizzle olive oil and lemon juice over the salad.
4. Season with salt and pepper to taste.
5. Toss gently and serve immediately.

Whole Wheat Pasta with Avocado Pesto

Ingredients:
- 8 ounces whole wheat pasta
- 1 ripe avocado, pitted and peeled
- 1/4 cup fresh basil leaves
- 1 clove garlic
- 2 tablespoons olive oil
- 2 tablespoons lemon juice
- 1/4 cup grated Parmesan cheese (optional)
- Salt and pepper, to taste

Instructions:
1. Cook whole wheat pasta according to package instructions. Drain and set aside.
2. In a blender, combine avocado, basil, garlic, olive oil, lemon juice, salt, and pepper. Blend until smooth.
3. Toss the cooked pasta with the avocado pesto.
4. Sprinkle with Parmesan cheese if desired.
5. Serve warm or chilled.

Red Lentil and Carrot Soup

Ingredients:
- 1 cup red lentils, rinsed
- 4 carrots, peeled and chopped
- 1 onion, chopped
- 2 cloves garlic, minced
- 4 cups vegetable broth
- 1 teaspoon cumin
- 1/2 teaspoon turmeric
- Salt and pepper, to taste
- Fresh cilantro, for garnish

Instructions:
1. In a large pot, sauté onion and garlic until softened.
2. Add carrots, lentils, cumin, turmeric, salt, and pepper.
3. Pour in vegetable broth and bring to a boil.
4. Reduce heat and simmer for 20-25 minutes until lentils and carrots are tender.
5. Blend the soup until smooth or leave it chunky, as desired.
6. Garnish with fresh cilantro and serve warm.

Farro Salad with Sun-Dried Tomatoes and Olives

Ingredients:
- 1 cup farro, cooked and cooled
- 1/4 cup sun-dried tomatoes, chopped
- 1/4 cup Kalamata olives, sliced
- 1/4 cup feta cheese, crumbled (optional)
- 2 tablespoons fresh parsley, chopped
- 2 tablespoons olive oil
- 1 tablespoon balsamic vinegar
- Salt and pepper, to taste

Instructions:
1. In a large bowl, combine cooked farro, sun-dried tomatoes, olives, and feta cheese.
2. Add chopped parsley, olive oil, and balsamic vinegar.
3. Toss the salad until all ingredients are well mixed.
4. Season with salt and pepper to taste.
5. Serve chilled or at room temperature.

Turkey Wrap with Guacamole and Tomatoes

Ingredients:
- 4 wholegrain tortillas
- 8 ounces cooked turkey breast, sliced
- 1/2 cup guacamole
- 1 tomato, sliced
- 1/2 cup lettuce, shredded
- Salt and pepper, to taste

Instructions:
1. Lay the tortillas flat and spread a layer of guacamole on each.
2. Add slices of turkey breast on top of the guacamole.
3. Layer with tomato slices and shredded lettuce.
4. Season with salt and pepper to taste.
5. Roll up the tortillas tightly to form wraps and serve immediately.

Brown Rice Bowl with Tofu and Vegetables

Ingredients:
- 1 cup brown rice, cooked
- 8 ounces firm tofu, cubed
- 1 cup broccoli florets
- 1 carrot, julienned
- 1 tablespoon soy sauce
- 1 tablespoon sesame oil
- 1 teaspoon ginger, minced
- 1 green onion, sliced
- Sesame seeds for garnish

Instructions:
1. In a pan, heat sesame oil and sauté tofu cubes until golden.
2. Add broccoli, carrot, and ginger; cook until vegetables are tender.
3. Stir in soy sauce and cook for an additional 2 minutes.
4. In a bowl, layer brown rice, sautéed tofu, and vegetables.
5. Top with sliced green onion and sesame seeds.
6. Serve warm.

Barley Salad with Vegetables and Feta Cheese

Ingredients:
- 1 cup pearl barley, cooked and cooled
- 1/2 cup cherry tomatoes, halved
- 1/2 cucumber, diced
- 1/4 cup red bell pepper, diced
- 1/4 cup crumbled feta cheese
- 2 tablespoons fresh parsley, chopped
- 2 tablespoons olive oil
- 1 tablespoon lemon juice
- Salt and pepper, to taste

Instructions:
1. In a large bowl, combine cooked barley, cherry tomatoes, cucumber, and red bell pepper.
2. Add crumbled feta cheese and chopped parsley.
3. Drizzle with olive oil and lemon juice.
4. Toss everything together and season with salt and pepper.
5. Serve chilled or at room temperature.

Chickpea and Spinach Salad with Lemon-Tahini Dressing

Ingredients:
- 1 can (15 oz) chickpeas, drained and rinsed

- 2 cups fresh spinach leaves
- 1/4 red onion, thinly sliced
- 1/4 cup cherry tomatoes, halved
- 1/4 cup tahini
- 2 tablespoons lemon juice
- 1 clove garlic, minced
- 2 tablespoons water
- Salt and pepper, to taste

Instructions:
1. In a large bowl, combine chickpeas, spinach, red onion, and cherry tomatoes.
2. In a small bowl, whisk together tahini, lemon juice, garlic, and water until smooth.
3. Drizzle the dressing over the salad and toss to combine.
4. Season with salt and pepper to taste.
5. Serve immediately.

Lentil and Roasted Vegetable Salad

Ingredients:
- 1 cup cooked lentils
- 1 zucchini, chopped
- 1 red bell pepper, chopped
- 1 carrot, chopped
- 1/4 cup red onion, sliced
- 2 tablespoons olive oil
- 1 tablespoon balsamic vinegar
- 1 teaspoon dried thyme
- Salt and pepper, to taste

Instructions:
1. Preheat the oven to 400°F (200°C). Toss zucchini, bell pepper, carrot, and red onion with olive oil, salt, and pepper.
2. Roast vegetables for 20-25 minutes until tender.
3. In a large bowl, combine cooked lentils with roasted vegetables.
4. Drizzle with balsamic vinegar and sprinkle with dried thyme.
5. Toss well and serve warm or chilled.

Turkey and Avocado Salad

Ingredients:
- 2 cups mixed greens
- 4 ounces cooked turkey breast, sliced
- 1 avocado, sliced
- 1/2 cucumber, sliced
- 1/4 cup cherry tomatoes, halved
- 2 tablespoons olive oil
- 1 tablespoon lemon juice
- Salt and pepper, to taste

Instructions:
1. In a large bowl, arrange mixed greens as the base.
2. Top with sliced turkey, avocado, cucumber, and cherry tomatoes.
3. Drizzle with olive oil and lemon juice.
4. Toss gently to combine and season with salt and pepper.
5. Serve immediately.

4.3 Batch Cooking for Lunches

Batch cooking is a practical and efficient strategy that can make your weekday lunches both healthy and convenient. By preparing large quantities of food in advance, you can save time during the week, reduce stress, and ensure that you always have nutritious meals ready to go. This approach is particularly useful for those with busy schedules, as it minimizes the need for daily cooking and helps you stick to a healthy eating plan.

In this section, we'll explore the benefits of batch cooking and provide tips and recipes for preparing lunches that can be stored and enjoyed throughout the week.

Benefits of Batch Cooking

Batch cooking offers several advantages that make it an ideal approach for meal prepping, especially for lunches:

- Time-Saving: Cooking in large batches allows you to prepare multiple meals in one cooking session, reducing the time spent in the kitchen during the week. Instead of cooking from scratch every day, you can simply reheat or assemble your pre-cooked components.

- Consistency: Having ready-made lunches ensures that you stick to your healthy eating plan, avoiding the temptation of fast food or unhealthy snacks. Batch cooking also makes portion control easier, as you can pre-portion meals according to your dietary needs.

- Cost-Effective: Buying ingredients in bulk for batch cooking can be more economical. It also reduces food waste, as you're more likely to use up all the ingredients you've purchased.

- Reduced Stress: Knowing that your lunches are prepared and ready to go can significantly reduce the stress of daily meal planning and cooking, giving you more time to focus on other important tasks.

Tips for Successful Batch Cooking

To make the most out of batch cooking, it's essential to plan and organize your cooking sessions effectively. Here are some tips to help you get started:

1. Plan Your Meals: Before you begin, decide on the meals you want to prepare for the week. Choose recipes that store well and reheat easily. Consider meals that can be varied by adding different toppings or sides to keep things interesting.

2. Choose Versatile Ingredients: Select ingredients that can be used in multiple dishes. For example, roasted vegetables can be added to salads, grain bowls, or wraps. Grilled chicken can be paired with different sauces or incorporated into various types of meals.

3. Invest in Quality Storage Containers: Use airtight containers that are freezer-safe and microwaveable. Clear containers are helpful so you can easily see what's inside. Divided containers can also be useful for keeping different components separate until you're ready to eat.

4. Label and Date Your Meals: Label your containers with the name of the dish and the date it was prepared. This will help you keep track of when the food needs to be eaten and ensure that nothing goes to waste.

5. Cook in Phases: If you're preparing several different dishes, it can be helpful to cook in phases. For example, start by roasting vegetables and cooking grains, then move on to proteins. This approach helps you manage kitchen space and ensures that all components are ready at the same time.

6. Cool Food Properly Before Storing: Let your cooked food cool completely before sealing it in containers and storing it in the refrigerator or freezer. This prevents condensation from making your meals soggy and helps maintain the quality of the food.

7. Consider Freezing: Some meals, like soups, stews, and casseroles, freeze exceptionally well and can be stored for longer periods. Freezing individual portions can be a great way to ensure that you always have a healthy lunch option available, even on the busiest days.

Batch Cooking Recipes

Here are some recipes that are perfect for batch cooking and can be stored for lunches throughout the week:

1. Quinoa and Roasted Vegetable Bowls

Ingredients:
- 2 cups quinoa, cooked
- 1 zucchini, chopped
- 1 red bell pepper, chopped
- 1 eggplant, chopped
- 1 cup cherry tomatoes, halved
- 2 tablespoons olive oil
- 1 teaspoon garlic powder
- Salt and pepper, to taste

Instructions:
1. Preheat the oven to 400°F (200°C).
2. Toss the zucchini, bell pepper, eggplant, and cherry tomatoes with olive oil, garlic powder, salt, and pepper.
3. Spread the vegetables on a baking sheet and roast for 25-30 minutes, until tender and slightly caramelized.
4. Divide the cooked quinoa into meal prep containers and top with the roasted vegetables.
5. Store in the refrigerator for up to 5 days. Reheat before serving.

2. Chicken and Brown Rice Stir-Fry

Ingredients:
- 4 chicken breasts, diced
- 3 cups brown rice, cooked
- 1 cup broccoli florets
- 1 red bell pepper, sliced
- 1 carrot, julienned
- 2 tablespoons soy sauce
- 1 tablespoon sesame oil
- 1 teaspoon ginger, minced
- 1 garlic clove, minced

Instructions:
1. In a large pan, heat sesame oil over medium heat. Add ginger and garlic, sauté for 1 minute.
2. Add diced chicken and cook until browned and fully cooked.
3. Add broccoli, bell pepper, and carrot to the pan, cooking until the vegetables are tender.
4. Stir in soy sauce and cooked brown rice, mixing everything together until heated through.
5. Divide into meal prep containers and store in the refrigerator for up to 4 days. Reheat before serving.

3. Lentil and Sweet Potato Stew

Ingredients:
- 1 cup dried lentils, rinsed
- 2 sweet potatoes, peeled and diced
- 1 onion, chopped
- 2 cloves garlic, minced
- 4 cups vegetable broth
- 1 teaspoon cumin
- 1 teaspoon paprika
- Salt and pepper, to taste
- Fresh cilantro, for garnish

Instructions:
1. In a large pot, sauté onion and garlic until softened.
2. Add sweet potatoes, lentils, cumin, and paprika. Stir to combine.
3. Pour in vegetable broth and bring to a boil.
4. Reduce heat and simmer for 30-35 minutes, until lentils and sweet potatoes are tender.
5. Season with salt and pepper. Divide into containers, garnish with fresh cilantro, and refrigerate for up to 5 days or freeze for up to 3 months. Reheat before serving.

4. Turkey and Avocado Wraps

Ingredients:
- 8 wholegrain tortillas
- 1 pound cooked turkey breast, sliced
- 2 avocados, sliced
- 1 cup lettuce, shredded
- 1/2 cup hummus
- 1 tomato, sliced

Instructions:
1. Lay out tortillas and spread a layer of hummus on each.
2. Top with turkey slices, avocado, lettuce, and tomato.
3. Roll up each tortilla tightly and wrap individually in foil or plastic wrap.
4. Store in the refrigerator for up to 4 days. Enjoy cold or at room temperature.

5. Mediterranean Farro Salad

Ingredients:
- 2 cups cooked farro
- 1/2 cup Kalamata olives, sliced
- 1/2 cup sun-dried tomatoes, chopped
- 1/4 cup feta cheese, crumbled
- 2 tablespoons olive oil
- 1 tablespoon lemon juice
- Fresh parsley, chopped

Instructions:
1. In a large bowl, combine cooked farro, olives, sun-dried tomatoes, and feta cheese.
2. Drizzle with olive oil and lemon juice, and toss to combine.
3. Sprinkle with fresh parsley.
4. Divide into meal prep containers and refrigerate for up to 5 days.

Batch cooking these recipes ensures that you have a variety of nutritious lunches ready for the week. With a little preparation, you can simplify your lunchtime routine and maintain a healthy, balanced diet, even on the busiest days.

Chapter 5: Healthy and Satisfying Dinners

Dinner is more than just the final meal of the day; it plays a crucial role in your overall health and well-being. A well-balanced dinner provides the nutrients your body needs to repair and recover during the night, supports metabolic functions, and even influences the quality of your sleep. This chapter will explore the importance of a balanced dinner, examining how it affects your sleep and nighttime recovery, and providing insights into how to create satisfying evening meals that nourish both your body and mind.

5.1 The Importance of a Balanced Dinner

The choices you make at dinner can have a significant impact on how well you sleep and how effectively your body recovers overnight. A balanced dinner is one that includes a variety of nutrients, such as complex carbohydrates, lean proteins, healthy fats, and plenty of vegetables. These components work together to support your body's nighttime processes, ensuring that you wake up refreshed and ready for the day ahead.

Supporting Sleep with the Right Nutrients

One of the primary ways dinner affects sleep is through its influence on the production of hormones that regulate sleep cycles, particularly melatonin and serotonin. Melatonin is the hormone responsible for signaling to your body that it's time to sleep, while serotonin helps stabilize mood and contributes to feelings of relaxation.

Certain foods contain nutrients that promote the production of these hormones. For example, tryptophan, an amino acid found in turkey, chicken, and dairy products, is a precursor to serotonin and melatonin. Consuming foods rich in tryptophan at dinner can help your body naturally produce these hormones, supporting better sleep quality.

Complex carbohydrates, such as those found in whole grains, sweet potatoes, and legumes, also play a role in sleep regulation. They help increase the availability of tryptophan in the brain, which in turn promotes the production of serotonin and melatonin. Including a moderate portion of complex carbohydrates in your dinner can therefore contribute to a more restful night.

Magnesium, a mineral found in leafy greens, nuts, seeds, and fish, is another nutrient that supports sleep. Magnesium helps relax the muscles and calm the nervous system, making it easier to fall asleep and stay asleep. Including magnesium-rich foods in your dinner can enhance your sleep quality and support overall relaxation.

Promoting Nighttime Recovery

During sleep, your body goes through various stages of recovery, including repairing muscles, replenishing energy stores, and supporting immune function. A balanced dinner that includes lean proteins, healthy fats, and plenty of vegetables provides the building blocks your body needs for these processes.

Protein is particularly important for muscle repair and recovery. During the day, your muscles experience wear and tear, especially if you're physically active. At night, your body uses the protein consumed at dinner to repair these muscles and build new tissue. Lean proteins, such as chicken, fish, tofu, and legumes, are excellent choices for dinner, as they provide high-quality amino acids that are essential for recovery.

Healthy fats, found in foods like avocados, nuts, seeds, and fatty fish, are also important for recovery. These fats support the absorption of fat-soluble vitamins (A, D, E, and K) and help reduce inflammation, which is crucial for healing and repair. Including healthy fats in your dinner not only supports recovery but also provides long-lasting energy that can prevent nighttime hunger.

Vegetables are a vital part of a balanced dinner, offering a rich source of vitamins, minerals, and antioxidants. These nutrients help protect your cells from oxidative stress and support immune function, both of which are essential for nighttime recovery. Leafy greens, cruciferous vegetables, and brightly colored vegetables are particularly beneficial for their high nutrient density.

Balancing Blood Sugar Levels

Maintaining stable blood sugar levels throughout the night is crucial for uninterrupted sleep and optimal recovery. A dinner that is too high in simple carbohydrates or sugars can cause blood sugar spikes and crashes, leading to restlessness, waking up in the middle of the night, or even feelings of hunger before bed.

To avoid these issues, focus on including complex carbohydrates, lean proteins, and healthy fats in your dinner. These components help slow the absorption of sugar into the bloodstream, preventing spikes and crashes. For example, a dinner that includes grilled salmon, quinoa, and a side of roasted vegetables provides a balanced mix of nutrients that help maintain stable blood sugar levels.

It's also important to avoid overeating at dinner. Large, heavy meals can cause discomfort and disrupt sleep, as your body works overtime to digest the food. Instead, aim for a portion-controlled meal that satisfies your hunger without leaving you feeling overly full.

Timing and Portion Control

When you eat dinner can be just as important as what you eat. Eating too late at night can interfere with your body's natural sleep rhythms, as your digestive system remains active when it should be winding down. Ideally, dinner should be consumed at least two to three hours before bedtime. This allows your body to fully digest the meal, reducing the risk of indigestion or acid reflux, which can disrupt sleep.

Portion control is also crucial for a balanced dinner. Overeating at dinner can lead to feelings of sluggishness and discomfort, making it harder to fall asleep. Additionally, consuming too many calories at night can lead to weight gain, as your body's metabolic rate slows down during sleep.

To avoid these issues, aim for a dinner that includes moderate portions of protein, carbohydrates, and fats, alongside plenty of vegetables. This approach ensures that you get the nutrients you need without overloading your digestive system.

Creating a Relaxing Evening Routine

Dinner is not just about the food you eat; it's also an opportunity to create a relaxing evening routine that prepares your body and mind for sleep. The way you approach dinner can influence your overall sense of relaxation and well-being.

Start by setting a calm and pleasant environment for your evening meal. Avoid eating in front of screens or while working, as this can lead to mindless eating and prevent you from fully enjoying your food. Instead, focus on the sensory experience of eating—appreciate the flavors, textures, and aromas of your meal.

Practicing mindful eating during dinner can also promote relaxation. Take your time with each bite, chew slowly, and savor the food. This practice not only aids digestion but also helps you tune in to your body's hunger and fullness signals, preventing overeating.

Incorporating a post-dinner routine that promotes relaxation can further enhance your sleep quality. After dinner, consider engaging in activities that help you unwind, such as taking a short walk, practicing gentle yoga, or enjoying a cup of herbal tea. These activities signal to your body that it's time to wind down and prepare for sleep.

Examples of Balanced Dinners for Optimal Sleep and Recovery

To help you put these principles into practice, here are a few examples of balanced dinners that support sleep and nighttime recovery:

1. Grilled Chicken with Quinoa and Steamed Broccoli: This meal provides lean protein from the chicken, complex carbohydrates from the quinoa, and a variety of vitamins and minerals from the broccoli. The combination of these nutrients supports muscle repair, stabilizes blood sugar levels, and promotes relaxation.

2. Baked Salmon with Sweet Potatoes and Spinach: Salmon is rich in omega-3 fatty acids, which reduce inflammation and support brain health. Paired with sweet potatoes, which offer complex carbohydrates, and spinach, which is high in magnesium, this dinner is ideal for promoting restful sleep.

3. Tofu Stir-Fry with Brown Rice and Mixed Vegetables: Tofu provides plant-based protein and is an excellent source of tryptophan. Brown rice adds fiber and complex carbohydrates, while the mixed vegetables offer a range of vitamins and minerals. This meal is balanced and satisfying, making it perfect for an evening meal.

4. Turkey and Avocado Salad with a Side of Whole Grain Bread: Turkey is another great source of tryptophan, while avocado provides healthy fats that support recovery. The whole grain bread adds complex carbohydrates, helping to maintain stable blood sugar levels.

5. Lentil Soup with a Side of Whole Grain Crackers: Lentils are rich in protein and fiber, making them a great choice for dinner. Paired with whole grain crackers, this meal is light yet nourishing, promoting both satiety and relaxation.

5.2 Simple and Tasty Dinner Recipes

Recipe List:

Vegetable and Legume Soup

Ingredients:
- 1 onion, chopped
- 2 carrots, chopped
- 2 celery stalks, chopped
- 2 cloves garlic, minced
- 1 zucchini, chopped
- 1 cup diced tomatoes (canned or fresh)
- 1 can (15 oz) mixed legumes (chickpeas, lentils, beans), drained and rinsed
- 4 cups vegetable broth
- 1 teaspoon thyme
- 1 teaspoon paprika
- Salt and pepper, to taste
- Fresh parsley, chopped (for garnish)

Instructions:
1. In a large pot, sauté the onion, carrots, celery, and garlic until softened.
2. Add zucchini and cook for a few minutes.
3. Stir in the diced tomatoes, mixed legumes, thyme, and paprika.
4. Pour in the vegetable broth and bring to a boil.
5. Reduce heat and simmer for 20-25 minutes.
6. Season with salt and pepper to taste.
7. Garnish with fresh parsley before serving.

Baked Fish Fillets with Lemon and Herbs

Ingredients:
- 4 white fish fillets (e.g., cod, tilapia)
- 2 tablespoons olive oil
- 2 tablespoons fresh lemon juice
- 1 teaspoon dried oregano
- 1 teaspoon dried thyme
- Salt and pepper, to taste
- Lemon slices and fresh herbs, for garnish

Instructions:
1. Preheat the oven to 375°F (190°C).
2. Place fish fillets on a baking sheet lined with parchment paper.
3. Drizzle with olive oil and lemon juice.
4. Sprinkle with oregano, thyme, salt, and pepper.
5. Bake for 15-20 minutes, until fish is cooked through and flakes easily with a fork.
6. Garnish with lemon slices and fresh herbs before serving.

Chicken Curry with Brown Rice

Ingredients:
- 2 chicken breasts, diced
- 1 onion, chopped
- 2 cloves garlic, minced
- 1 tablespoon curry powder
- 1 teaspoon turmeric
- 1 can (14 oz) coconut milk
- 1 cup diced tomatoes
- 2 cups cooked brown rice
- Salt and pepper, to taste

- Fresh cilantro, for garnish

Instructions:
1. In a large pan, sauté onion and garlic until softened.
2. Add diced chicken and cook until browned.
3. Stir in curry powder and turmeric, cooking for 1 minute.
4. Add coconut milk and diced tomatoes, stirring to combine.
5. Simmer for 15-20 minutes until the chicken is fully cooked and the sauce thickens.
6. Season with salt and pepper to taste.
7. Serve over brown rice, garnished with fresh cilantro.

Vegetarian Tacos with Black Beans and Avocado

Ingredients:
- 8 small corn tortillas
- 1 can (15 oz) black beans, drained and rinsed
- 1 avocado, sliced
- 1/2 cup red cabbage, shredded
- 1/2 cup corn kernels (fresh or canned)
- 1/4 cup red onion, finely chopped
- 1 lime, juiced
- 1 tablespoon olive oil
- Salt and pepper, to taste
- Fresh cilantro, for garnish

Instructions:
1. Heat the black beans in a pan with olive oil, salt, and pepper until warmed through.
2. Warm the tortillas in a separate pan or microwave.
3. Assemble the tacos by layering black beans, avocado slices, red cabbage, corn, and red onion on each tortilla.

4. Drizzle with lime juice and garnish with fresh cilantro.
5. Serve immediately.

Quinoa with Stir-Fried Vegetables and Tofu

Ingredients:
- 1 cup quinoa, cooked
- 8 oz firm tofu, cubed
- 1 bell pepper, sliced
- 1 zucchini, sliced
- 1 carrot, julienned
- 2 tablespoons soy sauce
- 1 tablespoon sesame oil
- 1 teaspoon ginger, minced
- 1 garlic clove, minced
- Green onions, for garnish

Instructions:
1. In a pan, heat sesame oil and sauté tofu until golden brown.
2. Add ginger and garlic, then stir in bell pepper, zucchini, and carrot.
3. Cook until vegetables are tender, then stir in soy sauce.
4. Serve stir-fried vegetables and tofu over cooked quinoa.
5. Garnish with green onions.

Kale Salad with Grilled Chicken and Almonds

Ingredients:
- 2 cups kale, chopped
- 1 grilled chicken breast, sliced
- 1/4 cup sliced almonds
- 1/4 cup dried cranberries
- 2 tablespoons olive oil
- 1 tablespoon balsamic vinegar
- Salt and pepper, to taste

Instructions:
1. In a large bowl, massage kale with olive oil until tender.
2. Add sliced grilled chicken, almonds, and cranberries.
3. Drizzle with balsamic vinegar, and season with salt and pepper.
4. Toss to combine and serve immediately.

Grilled Salmon with Asparagus and Sweet Potatoes

Ingredients:
- 4 salmon fillets
- 1 bunch asparagus, trimmed
- 2 large sweet potatoes, peeled and cubed
- 3 tablespoons olive oil
- 1 tablespoon lemon juice
- 1 teaspoon garlic powder
- Salt and pepper, to taste
- Fresh parsley, for garnish

Instructions:
1. Preheat the oven to 400°F (200°C). Toss sweet potatoes with 1 tablespoon olive oil, salt, and pepper. Roast for 25-30 minutes until tender.
2. Drizzle asparagus with 1 tablespoon olive oil, season with salt and pepper, and add to the oven for the last 10-15 minutes.
3. Preheat a grill or grill pan over medium heat. Brush salmon with remaining olive oil, lemon juice, garlic powder, salt, and pepper.
4. Grill salmon for 4-5 minutes per side until cooked through.
5. Serve salmon with roasted asparagus and sweet potatoes, garnished with fresh parsley.

Beef Stew with Vegetables and Potatoes

Ingredients:
- 1 lb beef stew meat, cubed

- 3 potatoes, peeled and cubed
- 3 carrots, sliced
- 2 celery stalks, chopped
- 1 onion, chopped
- 4 cups beef broth
- 2 tablespoons tomato paste
- 1 teaspoon thyme
- Salt and pepper, to taste

Instructions:
1. In a large pot, brown beef stew meat over medium heat.
2. Add onion, carrots, celery, and cook until softened.
3. Stir in tomato paste, thyme, salt, and pepper.
4. Add potatoes and beef broth. Bring to a boil, then reduce heat and simmer for 1.5 to 2 hours, until beef is tender.
5. Serve warm.

Wholegrain Mushroom Risotto with Parmesan

Ingredients:
- 1 cup wholegrain rice or barley
- 8 oz mushrooms, sliced
- 1 onion, chopped
- 2 cloves garlic, minced
- 4 cups vegetable broth, warmed
- 1/4 cup Parmesan cheese, grated
- 2 tablespoons olive oil
- Salt and pepper, to taste
- Fresh parsley, for garnish

Instructions:
1. In a large pan, heat olive oil and sauté onions and garlic until softened.
2. Add mushrooms and cook until browned.
3. Stir in wholegrain rice or barley, cooking for 2 minutes.
4. Gradually add warm vegetable broth, one ladle at a time, stirring frequently until absorbed.
5. Continue until grains are tender, about 30-40 minutes.
6. Stir in Parmesan cheese, season with salt and pepper, and garnish with fresh parsley before serving.

Chickpea Curry with Spinach and Basmati Rice

Ingredients:
- 1 can (15 oz) chickpeas, drained and rinsed
- 1 onion, chopped
- 2 cloves garlic, minced
- 1 tablespoon curry powder
- 1 teaspoon turmeric
- 1 can (14 oz) coconut milk
- 4 cups fresh spinach
- 1 cup basmati rice, cooked
- Salt and pepper, to taste

Instructions:
1. In a large pan, sauté onion and garlic until softened.
2. Stir in curry powder and turmeric, cooking for 1 minute.
3. Add chickpeas and coconut milk, simmering for 10 minutes.
4. Stir in spinach and cook until wilted.
5. Season with salt and pepper.
6. Serve over cooked basmati rice.

Baked Sweet Potatoes with Black Beans and Avocado

Ingredients:
- 2 large sweet potatoes
- 1 can (15 oz) black beans, drained and rinsed
- 1 avocado, sliced
- 1/4 cup sour cream or Greek yogurt

- 1 teaspoon cumin
- Salt and pepper, to taste
- Fresh cilantro, for garnish

Instructions:
1. Preheat oven to 400°F (200°C). Pierce sweet potatoes with a fork and bake for 45-50 minutes until tender.
2. In a pan, warm black beans with cumin, salt, and pepper.
3. Slice baked sweet potatoes open and fill with black beans and avocado.
4. Top with sour cream and garnish with fresh cilantro.

Stuffed Bell Peppers with Quinoa and Black Beans

Ingredients:
- 4 bell peppers, tops removed and seeded
- 1 cup cooked quinoa
- 1 can (15 oz) black beans, drained and rinsed
- 1 cup corn kernels
- 1/2 cup shredded cheese (optional)
- 1 teaspoon chili powder
- Salt and pepper, to taste

Instructions:
1. Preheat oven to 375°F (190°C).
2. In a bowl, mix cooked quinoa, black beans, corn, chili powder, salt, and pepper.
3. Stuff each bell pepper with the mixture and place in a baking dish.
4. Top with shredded cheese if desired.
5. Bake for 25-30 minutes until peppers are tender.

Grilled Shrimp Skewers with Garlic and Lemon

Ingredients:
- 1 lb shrimp, peeled and deveined
- 3 cloves garlic, minced
- 2 tablespoons olive oil
- 1 tablespoon lemon juice
- Salt and pepper, to taste
- Lemon wedges, for serving

Instructions:
1. Preheat grill to medium heat.
2. In a bowl, toss shrimp with garlic, olive oil, lemon juice, salt, and pepper.
3. Thread shrimp onto skewers.
4. Grill shrimp skewers for 2-3 minutes per side until pink and cooked through.
5. Serve with lemon wedges.

Chapter 6: Healthy and Easy Snacks

Snacking often gets a bad reputation, primarily due to the association with unhealthy, processed foods that offer little nutritional value. However, when done right, snacking can be an essential component of a healthy diet, especially for those with busy lifestyles or specific nutritional needs. A well-timed, nutritious snack can help keep your metabolism active, stabilize blood sugar levels, and prevent overeating during meals. In this chapter, we'll explore the importance of snacking, how it supports metabolic health, and how to choose snacks that contribute positively to your overall well-being.

6.1 The Need for Snacks During the Day

Snacking plays a crucial role in maintaining energy levels and supporting your body's metabolic processes throughout the day. While the traditional three-meals-a-day approach works for some, others may find that incorporating snacks between meals helps maintain focus, productivity, and overall energy. Here's why snacks are important and how they can be a beneficial part of your daily routine.

Supporting Metabolism

Metabolism refers to the processes your body uses to convert food into energy. It's an ongoing cycle that requires consistent fuel to function efficiently. When you eat, your body breaks down the food into glucose, which is then used to power everything from your brain to your muscles. The body's metabolic rate—the speed at which it burns calories—can be influenced by how often and what you eat.

Eating frequent, smaller meals or snacks can help keep your metabolism active throughout the day. When you go too long without eating, your body may start to conserve energy by slowing down your metabolism. This is a survival mechanism designed to protect you during periods of scarcity. However, in the modern world, where food is generally abundant, this slowdown can lead to decreased energy levels and, over time, weight gain. By eating small, nutritious snacks between meals, you help keep your metabolism engaged, promoting steady energy levels and supporting weight management.

Stabilizing Blood Sugar Levels

Another important reason to snack is to stabilize blood sugar levels. Blood sugar, or glucose, is the body's primary source of energy. After eating a meal, your blood sugar levels rise as glucose enters the bloodstream. Insulin, a hormone produced by the pancreas, helps cells absorb glucose for energy or storage.

However, after a few hours without food, blood sugar levels can drop, leading to feelings of fatigue, irritability, and difficulty concentrating.

Healthy snacks that include a balance of carbohydrates, proteins, and fats can help maintain stable blood sugar levels between meals. Carbohydrates provide a quick source of energy, while proteins and fats slow the absorption of glucose, preventing sharp spikes and crashes in blood sugar. This balance is crucial for maintaining consistent energy levels and avoiding the negative effects of blood sugar fluctuations, such as cravings for sugary or high-calorie foods.

For example, a snack like apple slices with almond butter offers a combination of carbohydrates from the apple and healthy fats and protein from the almond butter. This combination helps to keep blood sugar levels stable, providing sustained energy and preventing hunger until your next meal.

Preventing Overeating

One of the benefits of incorporating snacks into your day is that they can help prevent overeating at main meals. When you allow yourself to get too hungry between meals, you're more likely to overeat when you finally do sit down to eat. This is because your body, sensing that it needs to make up for lost energy, triggers a stronger hunger response, which can lead to consuming more calories than necessary.

By eating a small, nutritious snack a couple of hours before a meal, you can take the edge off your hunger. This makes it easier to control portion sizes during your main meals, reducing the likelihood of overeating. Snacks can also help satisfy specific cravings in a healthier way, making it less tempting to indulge in high-calorie, nutrient-poor options later in the day.

For example, if you have a craving for something sweet, a small serving of Greek yogurt with a handful of berries can satisfy your sweet tooth while providing protein, fiber, and antioxidants, all of which contribute to a healthy diet.

Maintaining Energy and Focus

Many people experience a dip in energy levels in the late afternoon, often referred to as the "afternoon slump." This is a natural part of the body's circadian rhythm, but it can be exacerbated by going too long without eating. A well-timed snack can help bridge the gap between lunch and dinner, providing the energy needed to stay focused and productive throughout the day.

Choosing snacks that are rich in nutrients can also help improve cognitive function and mood.

For instance, snacks that include omega-3 fatty acids, like walnuts or chia seeds, can support brain health, while those rich in fiber and protein can help you feel fuller for longer, reducing the temptation to reach for less healthy options.

Choosing the Right Snacks

The key to effective snacking is choosing the right foods. Not all snacks are created equal, and it's important to select options that provide real nutritional benefits rather than empty calories. Here are some tips for choosing healthy snacks:

- Focus on Whole Foods: Opt for snacks that are made from whole, minimally processed ingredients. Fresh fruits, vegetables, nuts, seeds, and whole grains are all excellent choices that provide essential vitamins, minerals, and antioxidants.

- Balance Macronutrients: Aim to include a mix of carbohydrates, proteins, and healthy fats in your snacks. This balance helps maintain steady energy levels and keeps you satisfied between meals.

- Watch Portion Sizes: Even healthy snacks can contribute to weight gain if eaten in large quantities. Pay attention to portion sizes and try to stick to a single serving.

- Prepare in Advance: Having healthy snacks ready to go can make it easier to stick to your nutritional goals. Consider preparing snack-sized portions of nuts, cut-up vegetables, or homemade energy bars at the beginning of the week.

- Stay Hydrated: Sometimes, feelings of hunger are actually a sign of dehydration. Make sure you're drinking enough water throughout the day, and consider snacks like cucumbers or watermelon, which have a high water content.

Examples of Healthy Snacks

To give you some inspiration, here are a few examples of healthy snacks that are easy to prepare and packed with nutrients:

1. Hummus with Veggie Sticks: Pair hummus with carrot sticks, cucumber slices, or bell pepper strips for a crunchy, satisfying snack that provides fiber, vitamins, and healthy fats.

2. Greek Yogurt with Berries: Greek yogurt is high in protein, and when topped with fresh berries, it offers a delicious combination of protein, fiber, and antioxidants.

3. Almonds and a Piece of Fruit: A handful of almonds paired with an apple or pear provides a great balance of healthy fats, protein, and carbohydrates.

4. Cottage Cheese with Pineapple: Cottage cheese is rich in protein, and when combined with pineapple, it makes a sweet and tangy snack that's also high in vitamins and minerals.

5. Wholegrain Crackers with Avocado: Spread mashed avocado on wholegrain crackers for a snack that's full of fiber, healthy fats, and complex carbohydrates.

6.2 Quick Snack Recipes

Recipe List:

Energy Bars with Nuts and Seeds

Ingredients:
- 1 cup mixed nuts (almonds, walnuts, cashews), chopped
- 1/2 cup mixed seeds (sunflower, chia, flax)
- 1/2 cup rolled oats
- 1/4 cup honey or maple syrup
- 1/4 cup almond butter or peanut butter
- 1/2 teaspoon vanilla extract
- Pinch of salt

Instructions:
1. In a large bowl, combine chopped nuts, seeds, and oats.
2. In a small saucepan, warm honey or maple syrup and almond butter over low heat until smooth.
3. Stir in vanilla extract and salt, then pour the mixture over the dry ingredients.
4. Mix well until everything is evenly coated.
5. Press the mixture firmly into an 8x8-inch pan lined with parchment paper.
6. Refrigerate for at least 2 hours before cutting into bars.
7. Store in an airtight container for up to one week.

Chickpea Hummus with Raw Vegetables

Ingredients:
- 1 can (15 oz) chickpeas, drained and rinsed
- 2 tablespoons tahini
- 2 tablespoons lemon juice
- 1 clove garlic, minced
- 2 tablespoons olive oil
- Salt and pepper, to taste
- Raw vegetables (carrots, celery, cucumber) for dipping

Instructions:
1. In a food processor, blend chickpeas, tahini, lemon juice, garlic, and olive oil until smooth.
2. Season with salt and pepper to taste.
3. Serve with an assortment of raw vegetables for dipping.

Greek Yogurt with Honey and Nuts

Ingredients:
- 1 cup Greek yogurt
- 1 tablespoon honey
- 2 tablespoons mixed nuts (almonds, walnuts, pistachios), chopped
- 1 teaspoon chia seeds (optional)

Instructions:
1. Spoon Greek yogurt into a bowl.
2. Drizzle with honey and sprinkle with chopped nuts.
3. Add chia seeds if desired.
4. Serve immediately for a quick, protein-packed snack.

Trail Mix with Dried Fruits and Dark Chocolate

Ingredients:
- 1 cup mixed nuts (almonds, cashews, walnuts)
- 1/2 cup dried fruits (raisins, cranberries, apricots)
- 1/4 cup dark chocolate chunks or chips
- 1/4 cup sunflower seeds
- 1/4 cup pumpkin seeds

Instructions:
1. In a large bowl, combine mixed nuts, dried fruits, dark chocolate, sunflower seeds, and pumpkin seeds.
2. Mix well to evenly distribute the ingredients.
3. Store in an airtight container for a quick and healthy snack on the go.

Baked Kale Chips

Ingredients:
- 1 bunch kale, washed and thoroughly dried
- 1 tablespoon olive oil
- 1/2 teaspoon sea salt
- 1/4 teaspoon garlic powder (optional)

Instructions:
1. Preheat the oven to 300°F (150°C).
2. Remove the kale leaves from the stems and tear them into bite-sized pieces.
3. Toss the kale with olive oil, sea salt, and garlic powder if using.
4. Spread the kale evenly on a baking sheet lined with parchment paper.
5. Bake for 20-25 minutes, turning halfway, until the kale is crispy.
6. Let cool and enjoy immediately or store in an airtight container.

Parmesan and Herb Popcorn

Ingredients:
- 1/2 cup popcorn kernels
- 2 tablespoons olive oil or melted butter
- 1/4 cup grated Parmesan cheese
- 1 teaspoon dried herbs (oregano, thyme, or rosemary)
- Salt, to taste

Instructions:
1. Pop the popcorn kernels using an air popper or on the stovetop with olive oil.
2. In a large bowl, drizzle the popped popcorn with olive oil or melted butter.
3. Sprinkle with Parmesan cheese, dried herbs, and salt.
4. Toss to coat the popcorn evenly.
5. Serve immediately for a savory snack.

Banana Peanut Butter Protein Smoothie

Ingredients:
- 1 banana, frozen
- 1 tablespoon peanut butter
- 1 scoop vanilla protein powder
- 1/2 cup almond milk or milk of choice
- 1/4 cup Greek yogurt
- 1/2 teaspoon cinnamon (optional)
- Ice cubes (optional)

Instructions:
1. In a blender, combine the frozen banana, peanut butter, protein powder, almond milk, and Greek yogurt.
2. Blend until smooth and creamy.
3. Add cinnamon and ice cubes if desired, and blend again.
4. Pour into a glass and enjoy immediately for a protein-packed start to your day.

Mini Vegetable Frittatas

Ingredients:
- 6 large eggs
- 1/2 cup spinach, chopped
- 1/2 red bell pepper, diced
- 1/4 cup onion, finely chopped
- 1/4 cup shredded cheese (optional)
- Salt and pepper, to taste

- Olive oil or non-stick spray, for greasing

Instructions:
1. Preheat the oven to 350°F (175°C). Grease a muffin tin with olive oil or non-stick spray.
2. In a large bowl, whisk the eggs and season with salt and pepper.
3. Stir in the spinach, bell pepper, onion, and cheese if using.
4. Pour the egg mixture into the muffin tin, filling each cup about 3/4 full.
5. Bake for 18-20 minutes, or until the frittatas are set and lightly golden.
6. Let cool slightly before removing from the tin. Serve warm or store in the refrigerator for a quick breakfast or snack.

Coconut Chocolate Energy Balls

Ingredients:
- 1 cup oats
- 1/2 cup almond butter
- 1/4 cup honey or maple syrup
- 1/4 cup unsweetened shredded coconut
- 2 tablespoons cocoa powder
- 1/4 cup dark chocolate chips
- 1 teaspoon vanilla extract

Instructions:
1. In a large bowl, mix oats, almond butter, honey, shredded coconut, cocoa powder, and vanilla extract until well combined.
2. Stir in dark chocolate chips.
3. Roll the mixture into small balls, about 1 inch in diameter.
4. Place the energy balls on a baking sheet and refrigerate for at least 30 minutes to firm up.
5. Store in an airtight container in the refrigerator for up to one week.

Green Smoothie with Spinach and Pineapple

Ingredients:
- 1 cup fresh spinach leaves
- 1/2 cup pineapple chunks (fresh or frozen)
- 1/2 banana
- 1/2 cup coconut water or water
- 1/2 cup Greek yogurt or almond milk (optional for creaminess)
- 1 tablespoon chia seeds (optional)
- Ice cubes (optional)

Instructions:
1. In a blender, combine spinach, pineapple, banana, coconut water, and Greek yogurt or almond milk if using.
2. Add chia seeds and ice cubes if desired.
3. Blend until smooth and creamy.
4. Pour into a glass and enjoy immediately for a refreshing, nutrient-packed smoothie.

6.3 On-the-Go Snacks

The key to successful on-the-go snacking is preparation. By having healthy options readily available, you can avoid the temptation of vending machines, fast food, or sugary treats. Portable snacks should be easy to carry, mess-free, and require minimal refrigeration. Here are some practical tips and recipes to help you keep your energy levels up throughout the day, no matter where you are.

Choosing the Right Containers

Before diving into the recipes, it's important to consider how you'll transport your snacks. Investing in a few good-quality containers can make a big difference in maintaining the freshness and portability of your food. Here are some options:

- Reusable Snack Bags: These are great for dry snacks like nuts, seeds, or granola. They're lightweight, easy to clean, and come in various sizes.
- Small Airtight Containers: Perfect for dips, cut-up fruits, and vegetables, these containers keep food fresh and prevent leaks.
- Insulated Lunch Bags: If your snack needs to stay cool, an insulated bag with a small ice pack is a convenient way to keep things fresh.

With the right containers, your snacks will be easy to pack and access, ensuring that you always have healthy options on hand.

Portable Snack Ideas and Recipes

Here are some recipes and ideas for nutritious snacks that travel well and can be eaten on the go:

1. Energy Balls

Energy balls are one of the best on-the-go snacks. They're easy to make, packed with nutrients, and don't require refrigeration, making them ideal for busy days.

Ingredients:
- 1 cup oats
- 1/2 cup almond butter
- 1/4 cup honey or maple syrup
- 1/4 cup shredded coconut
- 1/4 cup dark chocolate chips
- 1 teaspoon vanilla extract

Instructions:
1. In a large bowl, mix all the ingredients until well combined.
2. Roll the mixture into small balls, about 1 inch in diameter.
3. Store in an airtight container at room temperature or in the fridge for up to a week.
4. Pack a few in a reusable bag for a quick, energy-boosting snack on the go.

2. Veggie Sticks with Hummus

Fresh vegetables with a dip like hummus make for a crunchy, satisfying snack that's easy to pack and eat on the go.

Ingredients:
- 1 carrot, cut into sticks
- 1 cucumber, cut into sticks
- 1 red bell pepper, sliced
- 1/2 cup hummus (store-bought or homemade)

Instructions:
1. Prep the veggie sticks in advance and store them in a small airtight container or snack bag.
2. Portion out the hummus into a small container.
3. Keep them in an insulated lunch bag with an ice pack if needed, and enjoy your veggies and dip wherever you are.

3. Trail Mix

Trail mix is a classic portable snack that provides a great balance of healthy fats, protein, and fiber. Customize it with your favorite nuts, seeds, dried fruits, and a little dark chocolate.

Ingredients:
- 1/2 cup almonds
- 1/2 cup walnuts
- 1/4 cup sunflower seeds
- 1/4 cup dried cranberries
- 1/4 cup dark chocolate chips

Instructions:
1. Combine all ingredients in a large bowl and mix well.
2. Portion out the trail mix into reusable snack bags or small containers.
3. Store at room temperature and take a portion with you for a convenient, nutritious snack.

4. Apple Slices with Nut Butter

Apples paired with nut butter make for a sweet, filling snack that's easy to transport. The combination of fiber and healthy fats will keep you satisfied until your next meal.

Ingredients:
- 1 apple, sliced
- 2 tablespoons almond or peanut butter
- 1 teaspoon cinnamon (optional)

Instructions:
1. Slice the apple and place it in an airtight container to prevent browning.
2. Portion the nut butter into a small container.
3. Sprinkle cinnamon on the apple slices if desired.
4. When ready to eat, dip the apple slices into the nut butter for a quick, delicious snack.

5. Greek Yogurt Parfaits

Greek yogurt parfaits are a nutritious snack that you can easily prepare in advance. Layer the ingredients in a small container or jar for a portable, protein-rich treat.

Ingredients:
- 1/2 cup Greek yogurt
- 1/4 cup granola
- 1/4 cup mixed berries

- 1 teaspoon honey

Instructions:
1. Layer Greek yogurt, granola, and mixed berries in a small container or mason jar.
2. Drizzle with honey.
3. Keep it cool in an insulated bag with an ice pack if necessary, and enjoy it as a refreshing snack.

6. Wholegrain Crackers with Cheese and Grapes

This combination provides a balanced snack with carbs, protein, and healthy fats. It's easy to pack and perfect for a quick bite during a busy day.

Ingredients:
- 6-8 wholegrain crackers
- 2 ounces cheese (cheddar, gouda, or your favorite)
- A handful of grapes

Instructions:
1. Portion out the crackers and cheese into a small container.
2. Add the grapes in a separate container or bag to keep them fresh.
3. Pack in an insulated lunch bag if needed to keep the cheese cool.

7. Hard-Boiled Eggs

Hard-boiled eggs are a fantastic source of protein and can be easily prepared ahead of time. They're portable and perfect for a quick snack.

Ingredients:
- 2 hard-boiled eggs
- Salt and pepper, to taste

Instructions:
1. Boil eggs for 9-12 minutes, depending on your desired level of doneness.
2. Cool, peel, and store in the refrigerator until you're ready to pack them.
3. Season with salt and pepper just before eating. Pack in an insulated lunch bag to keep cool.

8. Banana and Nut Butter Wrap

This snack is simple to prepare and easy to eat on the go. It combines the fiber from the banana with healthy fats and protein from the nut butter.

Ingredients:
- 1 wholegrain tortilla
- 1 banana
- 2 tablespoons almond or peanut butter

Instructions:
1. Spread the nut butter evenly over the tortilla.
2. Place the banana in the center and roll up the tortilla around it.
3. Wrap it in foil or a reusable snack wrap for easy transport.

Tips for On-the-Go Snacking

- Prep Ahead: Set aside time each week to prepare and pack your snacks. This makes it easy to grab a healthy option when you're in a hurry.
- Keep It Simple: Choose snacks that don't require utensils and are easy to eat with your hands.
- Balance Is Key: Aim for snacks that include a mix of macronutrients—carbs, protein, and fat—to keep you full and energized.
- Stay Hydrated: Don't forget to carry a water bottle with you. Staying hydrated is just as important as eating the right snacks.

In conclusion, healthy on-the-go snacks are all about preparation and smart choices. By having nutritious options ready to go, you can stay energized and satisfied throughout the day, no matter where life takes you. Whether you're at work, on a road trip, or simply running errands, these snacks will help you maintain a balanced diet and avoid unhealthy temptations.

Chapter 7: Meals for Family and Friends

Cooking for a family or a group of friends can be a rewarding experience, but it also presents unique challenges. Everyone has different tastes, dietary preferences, and sometimes even restrictions that must be considered when preparing meals. The key to success is creating dishes that are versatile, adaptable, and capable of pleasing a variety of palates. In this chapter, we will explore strategies for cooking meals that satisfy the whole family, offering practical tips on how to adapt recipes to ensure that everyone at the table enjoys their meal.

7.1 Cooking for the Whole Family

Family meals are an opportunity to bring everyone together, share a nourishing meal, and enjoy each other's company. However, with varying preferences and potential dietary restrictions, it can be challenging to find a meal that pleases everyone. By using a few simple strategies, you can create adaptable meals that cater to a wide range of tastes, making dinner time an enjoyable experience for all.

1. Start with Versatile Base Recipes

One of the most effective ways to satisfy everyone's tastes is to start with a versatile base recipe that can be customized to suit individual preferences. Base recipes are typically simple and neutral, allowing you to add or adjust ingredients to cater to different tastes. Examples of versatile base recipes include:

- Pasta Dishes: Start with a plain pasta and let each person add their preferred sauce, such as marinara, Alfredo, or pesto. Include a variety of toppings like grilled chicken, sautéed vegetables, or cheese, so everyone can create their own dish.

- Grain Bowls: Cook a large batch of a base grain like rice, quinoa, or farro, and provide a variety of toppings like roasted vegetables, grilled meats, beans, and sauces. Each family member can then build their own bowl according to their taste.

- Taco Night: Set up a taco bar with tortillas, various proteins (chicken, beef, beans), and a selection of toppings like lettuce, cheese, salsa, and guacamole. This allows everyone to create their own tacos, customizing them to their liking.

- Build-Your-Own Pizzas: Use store-bought or homemade pizza dough as a base and offer a variety of sauces, cheeses, and toppings. Each family member can design their own personal pizza, ensuring everyone gets exactly what they want.

2. Embrace Customizable Meals

Customizable meals are a great way to accommodate different tastes within a single dish. By offering a meal that can be adjusted at the table, you allow each person to control the flavors and ingredients they prefer. Some ideas for customizable meals include:

- Stir-Fries: Prepare a base stir-fry with vegetables and a neutral sauce. Serve with a variety of proteins like tofu, shrimp, or chicken, and allow family members to add their preferred protein to their portion.

- Salads: Start with a basic green salad and offer a variety of add-ins such as grilled chicken, hard-boiled eggs, nuts, seeds, cheese, and dressings. This way, each person can customize their salad to suit their tastes.

- Soups: Prepare a simple broth-based soup and provide a selection of add-ins like noodles, rice, vegetables, and proteins. Each family member can then build their own bowl, adding the ingredients they enjoy.

3. Cook with Dietary Preferences in Mind

If your family includes members with specific dietary preferences or restrictions, it's important to plan meals that accommodate those needs without sacrificing flavor or variety. Here are some tips:

- Vegetarian or Vegan Options: When cooking for vegetarians or vegans, offer plant-based proteins like beans, tofu, or lentils as alternatives to meat. Many recipes can be easily adapted by swapping animal products for plant-based ones. For example, use vegetable broth instead of chicken broth, or offer a dairy-free cheese option.

- Gluten-Free Alternatives: For family members who are gluten intolerant, provide gluten-free grains like quinoa or rice, and use gluten-free pasta or bread. Many recipes can be made gluten-free with simple substitutions, such as using almond flour instead of wheat flour.

- Low-Sodium Choices: If someone in your family needs to reduce their sodium intake, prepare meals with fresh herbs and spices for flavor instead of relying on salt. Offer sauces and condiments on the side so that those who need to control their sodium can do so easily.

- Picky Eaters: For picky eaters, consider deconstructing meals into their individual components. For example, instead of serving a fully assembled casserole, serve the ingredients separately so each person can choose what they like. Offering familiar foods alongside new ones can also encourage picky eaters to try something different without feeling overwhelmed.

4. Incorporate Family Favorites

Every family has its favorite dishes, so be sure to include these in your meal rotation. Whether it's a beloved spaghetti recipe, a classic roast chicken, or a comforting mac and cheese, incorporating family favorites into your meal planning helps ensure that everyone is satisfied. You can also try introducing new variations of these favorites, such as adding vegetables to mac and cheese or experimenting with different sauces for chicken, to keep things interesting while still pleasing everyone.

5. Encourage Family Involvement

Getting the whole family involved in meal planning and preparation can make dinner more enjoyable for everyone. When family members have a say in what's on the menu, they're more likely to be excited about the meal. Here are some ways to involve your family:

- Meal Planning Together: Sit down as a family and plan the week's meals together. Ask for input on what everyone would like to eat and try to incorporate those suggestions into your meal plan.

- Cooking Together: Involve family members in the cooking process. Kids can help wash vegetables, set the table, or assemble simple dishes. Older children and adults can take on more complex tasks like chopping ingredients or cooking on the stovetop. Cooking together not only makes the process more fun but also teaches valuable kitchen skills.

- Creating a Family Cookbook: Compile favorite family recipes into a cookbook. This can be a fun project that allows everyone to contribute their favorite dishes and share them with each other. It's also a great way to preserve family traditions and pass down recipes to future generations.

6. Keep It Simple

While it's important to cater to everyone's tastes, it's also important not to overwhelm yourself with overly complicated meals. Simple, straightforward recipes that use fresh, wholesome ingredients can be just as satisfying as elaborate dishes. Focus on quality over quantity and choose recipes that you feel confident preparing.

7.2 Shared Meal Recipes

Recipe List:

Vegetarian Lasagna with Eggplant and Zucchini

Ingredients:
- 2 medium eggplants, sliced
- 2 zucchinis, sliced
- 9 lasagna noodles, cooked
- 2 cups marinara sauce
- 2 cups ricotta cheese
- 1 1/2 cups shredded mozzarella cheese
- 1/2 cup grated Parmesan cheese
- 1 tablespoon olive oil
- Salt and pepper, to taste
- Fresh basil, for garnish

Instructions:
1. Preheat oven to 375°F (190°C). Drizzle eggplant and zucchini slices with olive oil, salt, and pepper. Roast for 15-20 minutes until tender.
2. In a baking dish, spread a layer of marinara sauce, followed by 3 lasagna noodles.
3. Layer with roasted vegetables, ricotta cheese, and a sprinkle of mozzarella.
4. Repeat layers, finishing with a layer of marinara and remaining cheeses.
5. Bake for 30-35 minutes until bubbly and golden.
6. Garnish with fresh basil before serving.

Roast Chicken with Potatoes and Rosemary

Ingredients:
- 1 whole chicken
- 4 large potatoes, quartered
- 3 sprigs fresh rosemary
- 4 cloves garlic, minced
- 2 tablespoons olive oil
- Salt and pepper, to taste
- Lemon wedges, for serving

Instructions:
1. Preheat oven to 400°F (200°C). Rub the chicken with olive oil, garlic, rosemary, salt, and pepper.

2. Arrange potatoes around the chicken in a roasting pan. Drizzle with olive oil and season with salt and pepper.
3. Roast for 1 hour and 15 minutes, or until the chicken is golden and cooked through.
4. Let rest for 10 minutes before carving. Serve with lemon wedges.

Baked Rice and Vegetable Casserole

Ingredients:
- 1 cup uncooked brown rice
- 2 cups vegetable broth
- 1 zucchini, diced
- 1 bell pepper, diced
- 1 carrot, diced
- 1/2 cup frozen peas
- 1 cup shredded cheddar cheese
- 1 tablespoon olive oil
- 1 teaspoon Italian seasoning
- Salt and pepper, to taste

Instructions:
1. Preheat oven to 375°F (190°C). In a large baking dish, mix rice, vegetable broth, zucchini, bell pepper, carrot, peas, olive oil, Italian seasoning, salt, and pepper.
2. Cover tightly with foil and bake for 45 minutes.
3. Remove foil, sprinkle with cheese, and bake uncovered for an additional 10-15 minutes until cheese is melted and bubbly.
4. Serve warm

Wholegrain Pizza with Grilled Vegetables and Pesto

Ingredients:
- 1 wholegrain pizza crust
- 1/2 cup pesto sauce
- 1 zucchini, sliced
- 1 red bell pepper, sliced
- 1 red onion, sliced
- 1/2 cup cherry tomatoes, halved
- 1 cup shredded mozzarella cheese
- 1 tablespoon olive oil
- Salt and pepper, to taste
- Fresh basil, for garnish

Instructions:
1. Preheat oven to 400°F (200°C). Toss zucchini, bell pepper, and onion with olive oil, salt, and pepper.
2. Grill the vegetables until tender and slightly charred.
3. Spread pesto sauce over the pizza crust.
4. Arrange grilled vegetables and cherry tomatoes on top, and sprinkle with mozzarella cheese.
5. Bake for 12-15 minutes until the cheese is melted and bubbly.
6. Garnish with fresh basil before serving.

Turkey Roast with Baked Vegetables

Ingredients:
- 1 turkey breast, boneless
- 4 large carrots, peeled and sliced
- 3 potatoes, quartered
- 2 onions, quartered
- 3 cloves garlic, minced
- 2 tablespoons olive oil
- 2 teaspoons dried thyme
- Salt and pepper, to taste

Instructions:
1. Preheat oven to 375°F (190°C). Rub turkey breast with olive oil, garlic, thyme, salt, and pepper.
2. Place turkey in a roasting pan, surrounded by carrots, potatoes, and onions.
3. Drizzle vegetables with olive oil, and season with salt and pepper.

4. Roast for 1 hour, or until turkey is cooked through and vegetables are tender.
5. Let the turkey rest for 10 minutes before slicing.

Potato and Cheese Pie with Salad

Ingredients:
- 4 large potatoes, peeled and thinly sliced
- 1 1/2 cups shredded cheddar cheese
- 1/2 cup milk
- 2 eggs, beaten
- 1 tablespoon butter
- Salt and pepper, to taste
- Mixed greens, for salad
- Olive oil and vinegar, for dressing

Instructions:
1. Preheat oven to 375°F (190°C). Grease a pie dish with butter.
2. Layer half of the potato slices in the dish and sprinkle with half of the cheese, salt, and pepper.
3. Repeat with the remaining potatoes and cheese.
4. In a bowl, mix milk and beaten eggs, then pour over the potatoes.
5. Bake for 45-50 minutes, until the top is golden and the potatoes are tender.
6. Serve with a side salad dressed with olive oil and vinegar.

Vegetarian Chili with Beans and Corn

Ingredients:
- 1 can (15 oz) black beans, drained and rinsed
- 1 can (15 oz) kidney beans, drained and rinsed
- 1 cup corn kernels (fresh or frozen)
- 1 onion, chopped
- 2 cloves garlic, minced
- 1 bell pepper, chopped
- 1 can (14 oz) diced tomatoes
- 2 tablespoons chili powder
- 1 teaspoon cumin
- Salt and pepper, to taste
- Fresh cilantro, for garnish

Instructions:
1. In a large pot, sauté onion, garlic, and bell pepper until softened.
2. Add diced tomatoes, black beans, kidney beans, corn, chili powder, cumin, salt, and pepper.
3. Stir well and bring to a simmer.
4. Cook for 20-25 minutes, stirring occasionally, until flavors are well combined.
5. Serve hot, garnished with fresh cilantro.

Zucchini Noodles with Walnut Pesto

Ingredients:
- 4 zucchinis, spiralized into noodles
- 1/2 cup walnuts
- 1/2 cup fresh basil leaves
- 1/4 cup Parmesan cheese, grated
- 2 cloves garlic
- 1/4 cup olive oil
- Salt and pepper, to taste
- Cherry tomatoes, for garnish

Instructions:
1. In a food processor, blend walnuts, basil, Parmesan, garlic, olive oil, salt, and pepper until smooth.
2. Toss zucchini noodles with walnut pesto until well coated.
3. Garnish with cherry tomatoes and serve immediately.

Seafood Risotto

Ingredients:
- 1 cup Arborio rice
- 1/2 pound mixed seafood (shrimp, mussels, squid)
- 1 onion, finely chopped
- 2 cloves garlic, minced
- 4 cups fish or vegetable broth, warmed
- 1/2 cup white wine
- 2 tablespoons olive oil
- 1/4 cup Parmesan cheese, grated
- Fresh parsley, for garnish

Instructions:
1. In a large pan, heat olive oil and sauté onion and garlic until softened.
2. Add Arborio rice and cook for 2 minutes, stirring constantly.
3. Pour in white wine and cook until absorbed.
4. Gradually add warm broth, one ladle at a time, stirring frequently until the rice is creamy and al dente, about 18-20 minutes.
5. Add mixed seafood and cook until just done, about 5 minutes.
6. Stir in Parmesan cheese and garnish with fresh parsley before serving.

Chicken Cacciatore with Polenta

Ingredients:
- 4 chicken thighs
- 1 onion, chopped
- 2 cloves garlic, minced
- 1 bell pepper, sliced
- 1 can (14 oz) diced tomatoes
- 1/2 cup chicken broth
- 1 teaspoon dried oregano
- 1/2 teaspoon thyme
- Salt and pepper, to taste
- 1 cup polenta
- 2 tablespoons olive oil
- Fresh parsley, for garnish

Instructions:
1. Heat olive oil in a large pan over medium heat. Sear chicken thighs until browned, then set aside.
2. In the same pan, sauté onion, garlic, and bell pepper until softened.
3. Add diced tomatoes, chicken broth, oregano, thyme, salt, and pepper. Stir well.
4. Return chicken to the pan, cover, and simmer for 30 minutes.
5. Meanwhile, cook polenta according to package instructions.
6. Serve chicken cacciatore over polenta, garnished with fresh parsley.

Vegetable Paella with Saffron and Peas

Ingredients:
- 1 cup Arborio rice
- 1 onion, chopped
- 2 cloves garlic, minced
- 1 bell pepper, sliced
- 1 zucchini, diced
- 1/2 cup peas (fresh or frozen)
- 1/4 teaspoon saffron threads
- 4 cups vegetable broth, warmed
- 1 tablespoon olive oil
- Salt and pepper, to taste

Instructions:
1. Heat olive oil in a large pan and sauté onion, garlic, and bell pepper until softened.
2. Add Arborio rice and saffron, stirring well.

3. Gradually add warm broth, one ladle at a time, stirring until rice is cooked and creamy, about 18-20 minutes.
4. Stir in zucchini and peas, cooking until vegetables are tender.
5. Season with salt and pepper and serve hot.

Baked Ziti with Spinach and Ricotta

Ingredients:
- 12 oz ziti pasta, cooked
- 2 cups marinara sauce
- 2 cups fresh spinach, chopped
- 1 cup ricotta cheese
- 1 cup shredded mozzarella cheese
- 1/4 cup grated Parmesan cheese
- 1 teaspoon Italian seasoning
- Salt and pepper, to taste

Instructions:
1. Preheat oven to 375°F (190°C). In a large bowl, mix cooked ziti, marinara sauce, spinach, ricotta, Italian seasoning, salt, and pepper.
2. Transfer to a baking dish and top with mozzarella and Parmesan cheese.
3. Bake for 20-25 minutes until cheese is melted and bubbly.
4. Serve hot.

Chicken Fajitas with Bell Peppers and Onions

Ingredients:
- 1 lb chicken breast, sliced
- 2 bell peppers, sliced
- 1 onion, sliced
- 2 tablespoons olive oil
- 1 teaspoon chili powder
- 1/2 teaspoon cumin
- 1/2 teaspoon paprika
- Salt and pepper, to taste
- Tortillas, for serving
- Lime wedges, for garnish

Instructions:
1. In a large pan, heat olive oil over medium heat. Add chicken and cook until browned.
2. Add bell peppers, onion, chili powder, cumin, paprika, salt, and pepper. Sauté until vegetables are tender.
3. Serve chicken and vegetables in tortillas with a squeeze of lime juice.

7.3 Involving Children in the Kitchen

Getting children involved in the kitchen may seem daunting at first, especially with younger kids who may need more supervision. However, with the right approach, it can become a rewarding and enjoyable experience for everyone. Here are some strategies to help make cooking with children a success.

1. Start with Simple Tasks

When introducing children to the kitchen, it's important to start with simple, age-appropriate tasks. Younger children can begin with basic activities like washing fruits and vegetables, stirring ingredients, or measuring out simple ingredients like flour or sugar. These tasks allow them to get hands-on experience without being overwhelmed.

For example, toddlers can help tear lettuce for salads, rinse vegetables, or pour pre-measured ingredients into a mixing bowl. Preschoolers might enjoy tasks like mashing potatoes, spreading sauce on pizza dough, or cracking eggs (with a little help). As children grow older, they can gradually take on more complex responsibilities, such as chopping softer vegetables (with supervision), operating the blender, or even following simple recipes.

By starting with tasks that are easy and manageable, children will gain confidence and a sense of accomplishment, encouraging them to take on more challenging roles in the kitchen over time.

2. Make it Fun and Engaging

To keep children interested in cooking, make the experience fun and engaging. One way to do this is by turning meal preparation into a game or creative activity. For example, you can create a "pizza night" where each child gets to design their own mini pizza with different toppings. Or, set up a "build-your-own-taco" station where they can assemble their tacos with various fillings.

You can also involve children in the planning process by letting them choose a recipe from a cookbook or online that they'd like to try. This gives them a sense of ownership and excitement about the meal they're helping to prepare.

Using fun tools and gadgets, like cookie cutters, colorful mixing bowls, or child-sized utensils, can also make the experience more enjoyable. Allowing children to be creative with food presentation—like arranging fruit slices into fun shapes or decorating cupcakes—adds an artistic element that many kids find appealing.

3. Teach Kitchen Safety

While it's important to make cooking fun, safety should always be a top priority when children are in the kitchen. Teaching kids about kitchen safety from the start helps prevent accidents and instills good habits that will serve them well throughout their lives.

Begin by teaching children about basic hygiene, such as washing their hands before handling food and after touching raw ingredients like eggs or meat. Explain the importance of keeping the kitchen clean to avoid cross-contamination.

Introduce children to the concept of "kitchen rules," such as not touching hot surfaces, using oven mitts, and being careful around sharp objects. Younger children should be supervised closely when using kitchen tools, and they should be taught how to properly handle and pass utensils, especially knives.

For older children who are learning to use knives, start with small, safe cutting tasks, like slicing soft fruits with a butter knife, and gradually progress to more challenging tasks as their skills improve. Always emphasize the importance of focusing on what they're doing, taking their time, and using tools correctly.

4. Encourage Exploration and Experimentation

The kitchen is a great place for children to explore new foods and flavors. Encouraging them to taste and experiment with different ingredients can help broaden their palate and make them more adventurous eaters.

Allow children to sample ingredients as they cook, and ask them what they think of the flavors. Encourage them to suggest additions or changes to recipes based on their preferences. For example, if a child enjoys a particular herb or spice, they can try adding it to a dish to see how it changes the flavor. This experimentation not only makes cooking more interactive but also helps children develop their own taste preferences and culinary creativity.

Experimenting with different cuisines is another way to broaden a child's food horizons. Introduce them to foods from different cultures and let them help prepare international dishes. This can be both educational and exciting, as children learn about the world through food.

5. Turn Cooking into a Learning Opportunity

Cooking offers numerous opportunities for children to learn valuable skills beyond just food preparation. Math skills can be practiced through measuring ingredients, counting, and timing. Reading and following recipes can improve literacy and comprehension. Science concepts can be explored by discussing how ingredients change when mixed, heated, or cooled.

You can incorporate these learning opportunities naturally into the cooking process. For example, ask children to help measure out flour for a recipe and discuss the different units of measurement. When mixing ingredients, talk about what happens when you combine baking soda and vinegar or how yeast makes dough rise.

Cooking together also offers opportunities to teach life skills such as patience, organization, and teamwork. Encourage children to clean as they go, organize ingredients before starting a recipe, and work together to complete tasks. These skills will not only help them in the kitchen but in many other aspects of life as well.

6. Create a Positive Environment

It's important to create a positive and supportive environment in the kitchen where children feel encouraged and appreciated for their efforts. Celebrate their successes, no matter how small, and be patient with mistakes. If something doesn't turn out as expected, use it as a learning opportunity rather than a point of frustration.

Encourage children to take pride in their work by allowing them to present the food they helped prepare. Whether it's setting the table, serving the dish, or simply explaining what they made, giving children a role in the final presentation helps boost their confidence and makes the experience more rewarding.

7. Make it a Regular Activity

Involving children in the kitchen should be a regular activity rather than an occasional treat. Consistency helps them build skills over time and fosters a love for cooking that can last a lifetime. Even if it's just one meal a week, setting aside time to cook together as a family can create lasting memories and strengthen family bonds.

In conclusion, involving children in the kitchen is a wonderful way to teach them important life skills, encourage healthy eating habits, and create cherished family moments. By starting with simple tasks, making the experience fun, and emphasizing safety, you can help children develop a love for cooking that will serve them well throughout their lives. Whether you're preparing a family meal or experimenting with new recipes, cooking together is an opportunity for learning, creativity, and connection that benefits the whole family.

Chapter 8: Special Occasion Recipes

8.1 Festive Meals and Special Occasions

How to Maintain Healthy Eating During Holidays

Holidays and special occasions are a time of celebration, often filled with indulgent meals and tempting treats that can make maintaining a healthy diet challenging. However, it is possible to enjoy festive meals while still prioritizing your health and well-being. This section will explore practical strategies and ideas for balancing holiday indulgence with nutritious eating, ensuring that you can savor the moment without derailing your wellness goals.

1. Planning Ahead

One of the best ways to ensure that you maintain a healthy diet during holidays is by planning ahead. When we think of holidays, many of us immediately associate them with large gatherings, buffets, or elaborate dinners. Without a plan, it's easy to overindulge. Preparing a few key dishes that are both delicious and nutritious can help you stay on track. Before the event, decide what meals or dishes you can offer or bring to the table. This gives you control over at least part of the meal, ensuring there are healthy options available.

For example, if you're attending a family gathering or a potluck, volunteer to bring a dish like a vibrant salad, roasted vegetables, or a protein-packed entrée that aligns with your health goals. By doing so, you provide yourself and others with a healthy alternative to calorie-dense foods that may be served. Additionally, knowing what's on the menu allows you to mentally prepare and set limits in advance, reducing the temptation to overeat.

2. Portion Control and Mindful Eating

During special occasions, the abundance of food and the celebratory atmosphere often lead to overeating. One effective strategy to counteract this is mindful eating, which involves paying attention to what and how much you are consuming. This includes being aware of your hunger levels, savoring each bite, and eating slowly enough to enjoy the flavors of the meal.

By practicing portion control, you can enjoy a variety of festive dishes without overloading your plate. Start by serving yourself smaller portions of high-calorie or indulgent items and larger portions of vegetables, lean proteins, and whole grains. When it comes to treats, indulge mindfully by choosing a small portion of your favorite holiday dessert rather than sampling every sweet option available. This approach allows you to enjoy the indulgent aspects of the meal without going overboard.

Additionally, take time to enjoy the company and conversation around you. Socializing during meals can help you slow down and focus on the experience rather than rushing through the food. Engaging in conversation can also prevent mindless snacking, as you'll be more focused on your surroundings than continuously grazing on appetizers or treats.

3. Incorporating Healthier Ingredients

Holidays don't have to mean abandoning your healthy eating habits altogether. In fact, with a few simple ingredient swaps, many traditional dishes can be transformed into more nutritious versions without sacrificing taste. When preparing festive meals, try incorporating healthier ingredients that still deliver flavor and satisfaction.

For instance, instead of using heavy creams or excessive amounts of butter in side dishes like mashed potatoes or casseroles, substitute with Greek yogurt, olive oil, or coconut milk. These alternatives provide creaminess while adding nutritional benefits like protein or healthy fats. Similarly, use whole grains such as quinoa, farro, or brown rice in place of refined grains like white rice or white bread. These grains offer more fiber, which helps with digestion and keeps you fuller for longer.

When it comes to desserts, consider using natural sweeteners like honey, maple syrup, or fruit purees instead of refined sugar. You can also boost the nutritional value of baked goods by incorporating ingredients like almond flour, oats, or flaxseed meal. These changes will add more fiber, protein, and healthy fats to your holiday treats.

4. Maintaining Balance and Moderation

It's important to remember that holidays are meant to be enjoyed, and that includes allowing yourself to indulge in your favorite foods. Rather than focusing on strict dietary rules or feeling guilty for indulging, aim for balance. If you know you'll be attending a big holiday dinner, consider eating lighter meals earlier in the day that are rich in vegetables and lean proteins. This way, you can enjoy a festive meal without feeling overly full or bloated.

Another way to maintain balance is to avoid skipping meals. Many people make the mistake of fasting all day in anticipation of a large holiday feast, which often leads to overeating once the meal is served. Instead, eat smaller, balanced meals leading up to the event to keep your metabolism active and prevent excessive hunger.

Incorporating physical activity into your holiday routine is also a great way to balance indulgence with wellness. Whether it's a brisk walk with family, a game of football in the yard, or a morning yoga session, staying active can help you manage stress, boost your energy, and prevent the sluggishness that often accompanies heavy holiday meals.

5. Creating a Health-Conscious Holiday Menu

When hosting a holiday gathering, you have the opportunity to create a menu that combines festive flavors with wholesome, nutritious ingredients. Start with appetizers that are light yet satisfying, such as vegetable platters with hummus, smoked salmon on whole-grain crackers, or stuffed mushrooms with spinach and feta. These options provide a healthy start to the meal and prevent guests from filling up on less nutritious snacks like chips or processed dips.

For the main course, focus on lean proteins like roasted turkey, grilled fish, or plant-based alternatives like lentil loaf or stuffed acorn squash. Pair these with hearty vegetable side dishes such as roasted Brussels sprouts, carrots, or sweet potatoes seasoned with herbs and spices. Instead of relying on sugary sauces or gravies, enhance your dishes with natural flavors like citrus, garlic, or balsamic vinegar.

Desserts can also be both indulgent and healthy. For example, a fruit tart with a nut-based crust or a flourless chocolate cake made with avocado or black beans can satisfy your sweet tooth without the excess sugar or empty calories. Offer a variety of options, including fresh fruit, dark chocolate, or yogurt parfaits with granola and berries for those who prefer lighter treats.

6. Hydration and Alcohol Moderation

Holiday celebrations often involve alcohol, which can add extra calories and contribute to dehydration. To maintain a healthy balance, it's important to stay hydrated throughout the day, especially if you plan to enjoy alcoholic beverages. Drinking water before, during, and after meals can help control your appetite and prevent overconsumption of rich foods.

If you choose to drink alcohol, moderation is key. Opt for lighter options like wine, champagne, or spritzers, and try to alternate alcoholic drinks with water or sparkling water. Be mindful of sugary cocktails, which can contain high amounts of empty calories. Instead, choose drinks with simple ingredients like a vodka soda with lime or a gin and tonic with a splash of cranberry juice.

By keeping alcohol intake in check, you can enjoy the celebratory aspect of the holiday without feeling sluggish or experiencing the negative effects of overindulgence.

7. Handling Social Pressure

It's common to encounter social pressure to indulge during holidays, whether it's from family members urging you to try every dish or the cultural expectation to indulge. While it's important to enjoy the festive spirit, it's also okay to set boundaries and prioritize your health.

Politely decline second servings or high-calorie dishes by expressing gratitude and explaining that you're satisfied with what you've eaten. If someone insists on offering dessert or another drink, feel free to take a small portion or decline with a smile. Remember, it's your choice to enjoy the holiday in a way that makes you feel good, both mentally and physically.

8.2 Special Occasion Recipes

Recipe List:

1. Carrot and Walnut Cake
Ingredients:
- 2 cups grated carrots
- 1 ½ cups flour
- 1 cup chopped walnuts
- ¾ cup sugar
- ½ cup vegetable oil
- 3 large eggs
- 1 tsp vanilla extract
- 1 tsp baking powder
- 1 tsp cinnamon
- ½ tsp baking soda
- ¼ tsp salt

Instructions:
1. Preheat oven to 350°F (175°C). Grease a cake pan.
2. In a bowl, mix flour, baking powder, baking soda, cinnamon, and salt.
3. In another bowl, whisk sugar, oil, eggs, and vanilla. Gradually add the dry ingredients.
4. Fold in grated carrots and walnuts.
5. Pour batter into the pan and bake for 35-40 minutes, or until a toothpick comes out clean.
6. Let the cake cool before serving.

2. Benedict Eggs Brunch with Yogurt Sauce
Ingredients:
- 4 poached eggs
- 2 whole wheat English muffins
- 4 slices of smoked salmon
- ½ cup Greek yogurt
- 1 tbsp lemon juice
- 1 tbsp chopped dill
- Salt and pepper to taste

Instructions:
1. Toast English muffins and top with smoked salmon.
2. Poach the eggs and place on the salmon.
3. For the sauce, mix yogurt, lemon juice, dill, salt, and pepper.
4. Drizzle yogurt sauce over the eggs and serve warm.

3. Fish Tacos with Mango Salsa

Ingredients:
- 4 small tortillas
- 2 fillets white fish (tilapia, cod)
- 1 mango, diced
- ½ red onion, chopped
- 1 lime
- 1 tbsp olive oil
- Salt, pepper, cumin to taste
- Fresh cilantro for garnish

Instructions:
1. Season fish with salt, pepper, and cumin. Sear in olive oil for 3-4 minutes per side.
2. Mix mango, red onion, lime juice, and cilantro for salsa.
3. Warm tortillas, place fish, and top with mango salsa.
4. Serve with extra lime wedges.

4. Fruit Tart with Almond Crust

Ingredients:
- 1 cup almond flour
- 2 tbsp coconut oil, melted
- 2 tbsp honey
- 1 tsp vanilla extract

- 1 cup mixed fresh fruit (berries, kiwi, etc.)
- ½ cup Greek yogurt

Instructions:
1. Preheat oven to 350°F (175°C). Mix almond flour, coconut oil, honey, and vanilla until combined.
2. Press the mixture into a tart pan and bake for 10-12 minutes until golden. Let it cool.
3. Spread Greek yogurt over the crust.
4. Arrange fresh fruit on top. Serve chilled.

5. Spinach and Goat Cheese Stuffed Chicken
Ingredients:
- 4 chicken breasts
- 1 cup fresh spinach, chopped
- ½ cup goat cheese
- 1 garlic clove, minced
- 1 tbsp olive oil
- Salt and pepper to taste

Instructions:
1. Preheat oven to 375°F (190°C). Cut a pocket into each chicken breast.
2. Mix spinach, goat cheese, and garlic. Stuff the mixture into the chicken breasts.
3. Season with salt and pepper, then sear the chicken in olive oil until browned.
4. Bake in the oven for 20-25 minutes until fully cooked.

6. Grilled Vegetables with Romesco Sauce
Ingredients:
- 1 zucchini, sliced
- 1 red bell pepper, quartered
- 1 eggplant, sliced
- 2 tbsp olive oil
- Salt and pepper to taste
- ½ cup Romesco sauce

Instructions:
1. Preheat grill to medium-high. Toss vegetables in olive oil, salt, and pepper.
2. Grill vegetables for 4-5 minutes per side until tender and charred.
3. Serve with Romesco sauce drizzled on top or as a dipping sauce.

7. Shrimp and Avocado Ceviche

Ingredients:
- 1 lb cooked shrimp, chopped
- 2 avocados, diced
- 1 tomato, diced
- ½ red onion, chopped
- 1 jalapeño, minced
- ¼ cup cilantro, chopped
- ½ cup lime juice
- Salt and pepper to taste

Instructions:
1. In a bowl, combine shrimp, avocado, tomato, red onion, jalapeño, and cilantro.
2. Pour lime juice over the mixture and toss gently to coat.
3. Season with salt and pepper.
4. Chill for 20-30 minutes before serving to allow the flavors to meld.

8. Coconut Milk Panna Cotta with Berries

Ingredients:
- 2 cups coconut milk
- 2 tbsp honey
- 1 tsp vanilla extract
- 1 tbsp gelatin
- ¼ cup water
- Mixed berries (strawberries, blueberries, etc.)

Instructions:
1. In a saucepan, heat coconut milk, honey, and vanilla over medium heat until warm.
2. In a separate bowl, dissolve gelatin in water.

3. Once coconut milk is warm, stir in the gelatin mixture until fully combined.
4. Pour the mixture into molds and refrigerate for 4-6 hours until set.
5. Top with fresh berries before serving.

9. Watermelon Salad with Feta and Mint
Ingredients:
- 4 cups watermelon, cubed
- ½ cup feta cheese, crumbled
- ¼ cup fresh mint leaves, chopped
- 2 tbsp olive oil
- 1 tbsp lime juice
- Salt and pepper to taste

Instructions:
1. In a large bowl, combine watermelon, feta, and mint.
2. Drizzle with olive oil and lime juice.
3. Toss gently to combine.
4. Season with salt and pepper. Serve chilled.

10. Chicken Skewers with Peanut Sauce
Ingredients:
- 1 lb chicken breast, cut into cubes
- 2 tbsp soy sauce
- 1 tbsp olive oil
- 1 garlic clove, minced
- ½ cup peanut butter
- 2 tbsp lime juice
- 1 tbsp honey
- ¼ cup coconut milk

Instructions:
1. Marinate chicken in soy sauce, olive oil, and garlic for 30 minutes.
2. Thread chicken onto skewers and grill for 5-7 minutes per side until fully cooked.
3. For the sauce, whisk together peanut butter, lime juice, honey, and coconut milk.
4. Serve the skewers with peanut sauce on the side for dipping.

Chapter 9: Recipes for Specific Diets

9.1 Vegan and Vegetarian Diets

The Importance of a Balanced Diet Even for Specific Dietary Regimes

Adopting a vegan or vegetarian diet can have numerous health benefits, including improved digestion, better heart health, and reduced risk of certain chronic diseases. However, like any diet, it is crucial to ensure that it is well-balanced and provides all the essential nutrients your body needs. A common misconception about plant-based diets is that they lack adequate protein or vital nutrients such as iron, calcium, and vitamin B12. While these nutrients are more readily available in animal products, a carefully planned vegan or vegetarian diet can offer all the necessary components for a healthy, energetic lifestyle. This chapter will focus on why balanced nutrition is key in these specific diets and how to achieve it through delicious, plant-based recipes.

1. Understanding Nutritional Needs in Vegan and Vegetarian Diets

A balanced diet, regardless of whether it includes animal products or not, revolves around ensuring adequate intake of macronutrients (proteins, carbohydrates, and fats) and micronutrients (vitamins and minerals). In vegan and vegetarian diets, certain nutrients that are commonly found in animal products need to be sourced from plant-based alternatives. Understanding these nutritional needs helps avoid deficiencies and ensures overall well-being.

- Protein: One of the most common concerns for individuals on a vegan or vegetarian diet is protein intake. While meat, poultry, and fish are well-known protein sources, plant-based foods such as legumes (beans, lentils, chickpeas), tofu, tempeh, seitan, quinoa, and edamame provide substantial amounts of protein. For vegetarians, eggs and dairy products are also excellent sources of protein.

- Iron: Iron plays a vital role in transporting oxygen in the blood. Non-heme iron, the type found in plant-based foods, is not as easily absorbed as heme iron from animal products. However, you can improve iron absorption by combining iron-rich foods like spinach, lentils, and chickpeas with foods high in vitamin C, such as citrus fruits, bell peppers, and tomatoes.

- Calcium: For bone health, calcium is essential. While dairy products are often seen as the primary source of calcium, there are many plant-based sources like fortified plant milks (almond, soy, or oat milk), tofu, chia seeds, kale, and broccoli. Including these foods in a vegan or vegetarian diet helps maintain strong bones and teeth.

- Vitamin B12: This vitamin is crucial for nerve function and blood cell production, but it is naturally found only in animal products. Vegans and vegetarians need to obtain B12 from fortified foods (like plant-based milk and breakfast cereals) or take a supplement to meet their daily needs.

- Omega-3 Fatty Acids: Omega-3s, important for heart and brain health, are commonly found in fish. Plant-based sources include flaxseeds, chia seeds, hemp seeds, and walnuts. Including these in your diet can help maintain a healthy balance of essential fatty acids.

2. Building a Balanced Plate for Vegans and Vegetarians

A well-rounded vegan or vegetarian plate should include a variety of foods to ensure all nutritional needs are met. When planning meals, it's helpful to consider the following components:

- Protein: Aim to include a high-quality plant-based protein in every meal. Quinoa, tofu, tempeh, beans, and lentils are excellent choices that can be used in a variety of dishes from salads to stir-fries.

- Healthy Fats: Plant-based diets can provide ample healthy fats through nuts, seeds, avocado, and olive oil. These fats not only add flavor but are essential for nutrient absorption and energy production.

- Fiber: Whole grains, fruits, vegetables, legumes, and nuts provide plenty of fiber, which supports digestion and helps regulate blood sugar levels. Incorporating a wide variety of these foods ensures you're getting enough fiber while also benefiting from their different micronutrients.

- Micronutrients: Keep an eye on nutrients like iron, calcium, and vitamin B12. Include fortified foods or consider supplements, especially for vitamin B12, to prevent deficiencies.

By focusing on diverse food choices and combining different sources of proteins, fats, and fiber, vegans and vegetarians can create satisfying, nutrient-dense meals that support their health and energy levels.

3. Common Challenges and How to Overcome Them

While a vegan or vegetarian diet can be incredibly healthy, it does come with certain challenges, particularly for those new to the lifestyle. A lack of preparation can lead to unbalanced meals that lack key nutrients. However, with a little knowledge and foresight, it's easy to overcome these obstacles.

- Protein Deficiency: One of the most common mistakes made by new vegans or vegetarians is not consuming enough protein. By incorporating a variety of protein-rich foods like beans, lentils, tofu, and whole grains into your diet, you can easily meet your daily protein needs. Combining foods such as rice and beans or peanut butter on whole-grain toast creates complete proteins, offering all essential amino acids.

- Iron Absorption: Since plant-based iron is not as readily absorbed as iron from animal sources, combining iron-rich foods with vitamin C-rich foods is essential. For example, pairing spinach with a lemon-based dressing or adding bell peppers to a chickpea salad will enhance iron absorption.

- Boredom with Meal Options: Some people worry that a vegan or vegetarian diet might be limiting. However, plant-based cooking offers a wide variety of ingredients and culinary possibilities. Experimenting with spices, herbs, and different cooking techniques can add excitement to your meals. Incorporating global cuisines, such as Indian curries, Middle Eastern falafels, or Mexican bean dishes, helps keep your meals diverse and flavorful.

4. Delicious Vegan and Vegetarian Recipes

Here are a few examples of easy, balanced, and delicious vegan and vegetarian recipes to inspire your cooking:

- Chickpea and Quinoa Burgers with Guacamole: These plant-based burgers are packed with protein from chickpeas and quinoa. Serve them with a dollop of fresh guacamole for a creamy, nutritious topping.

- Pumpkin and Ginger Soup: A comforting bowl of soup made from roasted pumpkin and a hint of ginger provides warmth and plenty of vitamins A and C. Pair with whole-grain bread for a complete meal.

- Wholegrain Couscous Salad with Chickpeas and Grilled Vegetables: This salad combines couscous, chickpeas, and a variety of grilled vegetables, providing a high-fiber, protein-rich dish that's both hearty and flavorful.

- Chocolate Avocado Mousse: For a sweet treat, this mousse combines creamy avocado and dark chocolate, offering a dessert that's rich in healthy fats and antioxidants.

- Zucchini Noodles with Pesto and Cherry Tomatoes: A fresh and light meal that replaces traditional pasta with zucchini noodles, topped with a flavorful basil pesto and juicy cherry tomatoes.

9.2 Vegan and Vegetarian Recipes

Recipe List:

Marinated Tofu with Stir-Fried Vegetables
Ingredients:
- 1 block firm tofu, cubed
- 2 tbsp soy sauce
- 1 tbsp sesame oil
- 1 garlic clove, minced
- 1 tbsp rice vinegar
- 1 zucchini, sliced
- 1 bell pepper, sliced
- 1 carrot, julienned
- 2 tbsp vegetable oil

Instructions:
1. Marinate tofu in soy sauce, sesame oil, garlic, and rice vinegar for 30 minutes.
2. Heat vegetable oil in a pan and stir-fry zucchini, bell pepper, and carrot for 5-6 minutes.
3. Add marinated tofu and stir-fry until golden brown.
4. Serve with rice or noodles.

Chickpea and Quinoa Burgers with Guacamole
Ingredients:
- 1 cup cooked quinoa
- 1 can chickpeas, drained
- 1 tsp cumin
- 1 garlic clove, minced
- 1 avocado
- 1 lime, juiced
- Salt and pepper

Instructions:
1. Mash chickpeas and mix with quinoa, cumin, garlic, salt, and pepper. Form into patties.
2. Cook patties in a pan with olive oil for 4-5 minutes per side.
3. Mash avocado with lime juice and a pinch of salt for guacamole.
4. Serve burgers with guacamole on whole-grain buns.

Pumpkin and Ginger Soup
Ingredients:
- 4 cups pumpkin, cubed
- 1 onion, chopped
- 1 tbsp fresh ginger, grated
- 3 cups vegetable broth

- 1 tbsp olive oil

Instructions:
1. Sauté onion and ginger in olive oil until soft.
2. Add pumpkin cubes and vegetable broth. Simmer for 20 minutes until pumpkin is tender.
3. Blend the soup until smooth and season with salt and pepper.
4. Serve warm, garnished with fresh herbs.

Wholegrain Couscous Salad with Chickpeas and Grilled Vegetables
Ingredients:
- 1 cup wholegrain couscous
- 1 can chickpeas, drained
- 1 zucchini, sliced
- 1 red bell pepper, sliced
- 1 tbsp olive oil
- 1 tsp cumin
- 2 tbsp lemon juice
- Fresh parsley, chopped

Instructions:
1. Cook couscous according to package instructions.
2. Grill zucchini and bell pepper with olive oil until tender.
3. In a bowl, mix couscous, chickpeas, grilled vegetables, cumin, lemon juice, and parsley.
4. Season with salt and pepper, and serve chilled or at room temperature.

Gluten-Free Protein Bread
Ingredients:
- 1 cup almond flour
- ¼ cup flaxseed meal
- ¼ cup protein powder
- 3 eggs
- 1 tsp baking soda
- 1 tbsp apple cider vinegar
- 2 tbsp olive oil

Instructions:
1. Preheat oven to 350°F (175°C). Grease a loaf pan.
2. In a bowl, mix almond flour, flaxseed meal, protein powder, and baking soda.
3. Whisk eggs, apple cider vinegar, and olive oil, then combine with dry ingredients.
4. Pour batter into the pan and bake for 30-35 minutes until a toothpick comes out clean.
5. Let cool before slicing.

Chocolate Avocado Mousse
Ingredients:
- 2 ripe avocados
- ¼ cup cocoa powder
- ¼ cup honey or maple syrup
- 1 tsp vanilla extract
- A pinch of sea salt

Instructions:
1. Blend avocados, cocoa powder, honey, vanilla extract, and sea salt until smooth.
2. Adjust sweetness if needed.
3. Refrigerate for 1 hour before serving.
4. Garnish with fresh berries or shaved dark chocolate.

Rice Pasta with Pistachio Pesto
Ingredients:
- 200g rice pasta
- 1 cup pistachios, shelled
- 1 cup fresh basil leaves
- 1 garlic clove
- ¼ cup olive oil
- 2 tbsp lemon juice
- Salt and pepper to taste

Instructions:
1. Cook rice pasta according to package instructions. Drain and set aside.
2. In a food processor, blend pistachios, basil, garlic, olive oil, and lemon juice until smooth.
3. Season with salt and pepper.
4. Toss the pesto with the cooked pasta.
5. Serve with extra chopped pistachios on top.

Kale Salad with Apples and Walnuts
Ingredients:
- 4 cups kale, chopped
- 1 apple, thinly sliced
- ¼ cup walnuts, toasted
- 2 tbsp olive oil
- 1 tbsp apple cider vinegar
- 1 tsp honey
- Salt and pepper to taste

Instructions:
1. In a bowl, massage the chopped kale with olive oil for 2-3 minutes to soften the leaves.
2. Add the sliced apple and toasted walnuts.
3. In a small bowl, whisk together apple cider vinegar, honey, salt, and pepper.
4. Drizzle the dressing over the salad and toss to combine.

Brown Rice Bowl with Tempeh and Vegetables
Ingredients:
- 1 cup cooked brown rice
- 100g tempeh, cubed
- 1 zucchini, sliced
- 1 carrot, julienned
- 1 tbsp soy sauce
- 1 tbsp olive oil
- 1 tsp sesame seeds

Instructions:
1. Sauté tempeh in olive oil until golden brown.
2. Add zucchini and carrots, stir-fry for 3-4 minutes.
3. Stir in soy sauce and cook for another minute.
4. Serve over brown rice, garnished with sesame seeds.

10. Flourless Chocolate Brownies

Ingredients:
- 1 cup almond butter
- ½ cup cocoa powder
- ¼ cup honey or maple syrup
- 2 eggs
- 1 tsp vanilla extract
- ½ tsp baking soda
- A pinch of sea salt

Instructions:
1. Preheat oven to 350°F (175°C). Line a baking pan with parchment paper.
2. In a bowl, mix almond butter, cocoa powder, honey, eggs, vanilla extract, baking soda, and sea salt until smooth.
3. Pour the batter into the prepared pan and spread evenly.
4. Bake for 20-25 minutes, or until a toothpick comes out clean.
5. Let the brownies cool completely before cutting into squares.

11. Cauliflower Rice Stir-Fry with Tofu

Ingredients:
- 1 block firm tofu, cubed
- 2 cups cauliflower rice
- 1 carrot, julienned

- 1 bell pepper, sliced
- 2 tbsp soy sauce
- 1 tbsp sesame oil
- 1 garlic clove, minced
- 1 tsp ginger, grated

Instructions:

1. Heat sesame oil in a pan and sauté tofu until golden brown. Set aside.
2. In the same pan, sauté garlic and ginger until fragrant.
3. Add the cauliflower rice, carrot, and bell pepper. Stir-fry for 5-6 minutes.
4. Stir in soy sauce and tofu. Cook for another 2 minutes.
5. Serve hot, garnished with sesame seeds if desired.

12. Zucchini Noodles with Pesto and Cherry Tomatoes

Ingredients:

- 2 zucchinis, spiralized into noodles
- 1 cup cherry tomatoes, halved
- ½ cup basil pesto (homemade or store-bought)
- 2 tbsp olive oil
- Salt and pepper to taste

Instructions:

1. Heat olive oil in a pan and sauté zucchini noodles for 2-3 minutes until slightly softened.
2. Add cherry tomatoes and cook for another minute.
3. Remove from heat and toss with basil pesto.
4. Season with salt and pepper, and serve immediately.

13. Eggplant and Mushroom Stir-Fry
Ingredients:
- 1 eggplant, cubed
- 1 cup mushrooms, sliced
- 1 tbsp soy sauce
- 1 tbsp rice vinegar
- 2 tbsp olive oil
- 1 garlic clove, minced
- 1 tsp sesame seeds (optional)

Instructions:
1. Heat olive oil in a pan and sauté the garlic until fragrant.
2. Add eggplant and mushrooms, cooking until tender (about 6-8 minutes).
3. Stir in soy sauce and rice vinegar, allowing the vegetables to absorb the flavors.
4. Cook for an additional 2 minutes, then remove from heat.
5. Garnish with sesame seeds and serve hot, either on its own or with rice.

9.3 Low-Carb and Keto-Friendly Recipes

Options for Those Following Low-Carb or Ketogenic Diets, with Recipes that Maintain High Nutritional Value

Low-carb and ketogenic diets have gained widespread popularity for their potential benefits in weight management, energy stabilization, and even supporting certain health conditions. These diets focus on reducing carbohydrate intake while increasing fat consumption, encouraging the body to enter a metabolic state known as ketosis, where fat is used as the primary energy source instead of glucose. However, like any diet, it is essential to ensure that meals are well-balanced and nutritionally dense, providing the body with the vitamins, minerals, and macronutrients it needs to function optimally.

In this chapter, we will explore the principles of low-carb and keto-friendly eating, the benefits of these diets, and how to create meals that are both satisfying and nutritious. Whether you're looking to reduce carbs or maintain a ketogenic lifestyle, these recipes offer high nutritional value without compromising flavor.

1. Understanding Low-Carb and Keto-Friendly Diets

A low-carb diet typically limits carbohydrate intake to between 20-100 grams per day, depending on individual goals and needs. It emphasizes consuming healthy fats, moderate protein, and plenty of non-starchy vegetables. The ketogenic (keto) diet takes carb restriction a step further, aiming to keep carbohydrate intake below 20-50 grams per day to trigger ketosis. In ketosis, the liver converts fats into ketones, which then become the primary fuel source for the body.

To succeed on a low-carb or keto diet, it is important to choose nutrient-dense, whole foods and avoid processed items high in sugar and refined carbs. The foundation of these diets includes:

- Healthy fats: Olive oil, coconut oil, avocado, butter, ghee, and fatty fish like salmon.
- Protein: Eggs, poultry, beef, pork, tofu, and plant-based options like tempeh (for those following plant-based keto).
- Non-starchy vegetables: Leafy greens, broccoli, cauliflower, zucchini, and bell peppers.
- Low-carb fruits: Berries, avocados, and small amounts of other low-sugar fruits.
- Nuts and seeds: Almonds, walnuts, chia seeds, and flaxseeds.

With careful planning, a low-carb or keto diet can provide a well-rounded intake of essential nutrients, including fiber, vitamins, and minerals, while keeping carbohydrate intake low.

2. The Benefits of Low-Carb and Keto Diets

The appeal of low-carb and ketogenic diets lies in their potential benefits for both body composition and overall health. Here are some of the advantages:

- Weight loss: Reducing carbohydrate intake leads to lower insulin levels, promoting the use of stored fat for energy. This can result in effective weight loss, particularly when paired with proper portion control and healthy food choices.
- Stable energy levels: Without the rapid blood sugar spikes caused by high-carb meals, many individuals report more consistent energy levels throughout the day on a low-carb or keto diet. Fat and protein provide a steady source of fuel, reducing energy crashes.
- Improved mental clarity: Ketones, which the brain uses as fuel in ketosis, may enhance cognitive function, leading to clearer thinking and better focus for some individuals.
- Support for metabolic conditions: The ketogenic diet has been shown to improve markers of metabolic syndrome, including insulin sensitivity, blood pressure, and cholesterol levels. It may also be beneficial for those with type 2 diabetes by reducing blood sugar and insulin spikes.
- Satiation and reduced cravings: High-fat and moderate-protein meals tend to be more satiating, which may help reduce hunger and cravings, making it easier to stick to the diet over time.

3. Creating Nutritionally Balanced Low-Carb and Keto Meals

Ensuring that your meals are both low-carb and nutritionally balanced requires a focus on variety and quality ingredients. Here are some strategies for creating well-rounded dishes:

- Incorporate plenty of non-starchy vegetables: Leafy greens, cauliflower, zucchini, and other low-carb vegetables should make up a significant portion of your meals. They provide essential vitamins, minerals, and fiber, which are critical for digestion and overall health.
- Choose high-quality fats: Fats are a central part of the keto diet, but not all fats are created equal. Opt for healthy fats like olive oil, avocado, and coconut oil, which provide anti-inflammatory properties and essential fatty acids.
- Don't forget about protein: While low-carb and keto diets are not high-protein diets, it's important to consume moderate amounts of protein to support muscle health and repair. Eggs, fish, poultry, and plant-based protein sources like tofu can be included regularly.
- Stay hydrated: Low-carb and ketogenic diets can have a diuretic effect, leading to increased fluid loss. Be sure to drink plenty of water and include electrolyte-rich foods like leafy greens and avocados to maintain proper hydration.

4. Low-Carb and Keto-Friendly Recipe Ideas

Zucchini Lasagna with Ground Beef

Ingredients:
- 2 large zucchinis, thinly sliced
- 1 lb ground beef
- 1 cup ricotta cheese
- 1 cup shredded mozzarella cheese
- 1 cup marinara sauce (no added sugar)
- 1 tbsp olive oil
- 1 garlic clove, minced
- Salt and pepper to taste

Instructions:
1. Preheat oven to 375°F (190°C).
2. Sauté garlic in olive oil, then add ground beef. Cook until browned.
3. Layer thinly sliced zucchini, ricotta, ground beef, and marinara sauce in a baking dish.
4. Top with shredded mozzarella cheese and bake for 20-25 minutes until golden and bubbly.

Cauliflower Pizza Crust

Ingredients:
- 1 medium head cauliflower, riced
- 1 egg
- ½ cup shredded mozzarella
- 1 tsp oregano
- Salt and pepper to taste

Instructions:
1. Preheat oven to 400°F (200°C).
2. Steam cauliflower rice until tender, then squeeze out excess water.
3. Mix cauliflower with egg, mozzarella, oregano, salt, and pepper.
4. Press mixture into a pizza shape on a parchment-lined baking sheet.
5. Bake for 15-20 minutes until firm, then add toppings of choice and bake for an additional 10 minutes.

Avocado and Bacon Salad

Ingredients:
- 1 avocado, diced
- 4 slices bacon, cooked and crumbled
- 2 cups spinach leaves
- 1 tbsp olive oil
- 1 tbsp lemon juice
- Salt and pepper to taste

Instructions:
1. In a bowl, toss spinach, avocado, and bacon.
2. Drizzle with olive oil and lemon juice.
3. Season with salt and pepper, and serve fresh.

Keto Chocolate Fat Bombs

Ingredients:
- ½ cup coconut oil
- ¼ cup cocoa powder
- 2 tbsp peanut butter (unsweetened)
- 1 tbsp stevia or low-carb sweetener

Instructions:
1. Melt coconut oil and peanut butter together in a small saucepan.
2. Stir in cocoa powder and sweetener until smooth.
3. Pour mixture into molds or a lined tray and refrigerate until set, about 1 hour.
4. Enjoy as a high-fat snack or dessert.

Stuffed Bell Peppers with Ground Turkey and Cheese

Ingredients:
- 4 bell peppers, tops removed and seeds scooped out
- 1 lb ground turkey
- 1 cup shredded cheddar cheese
- 1 onion, chopped

- 2 tbsp olive oil
- 1 tsp paprika
- Salt and pepper to taste

Instructions:
1. Preheat oven to 375°F (190°C).
2. Sauté onion in olive oil, then add ground turkey, paprika, salt, and pepper. Cook until browned.
3. Stuff each bell pepper with the turkey mixture and top with shredded cheese.
4. Bake for 20-25 minutes until the peppers are tender and the cheese is melted.

Conclusion

A low-carb or ketogenic diet doesn't have to be restrictive or lacking in variety. With a little creativity and attention to nutritional balance, these diets can be flavorful, satisfying, and highly beneficial for overall health. By focusing on whole foods like vegetables, healthy fats, and quality proteins, you can enjoy delicious meals that align with your low-carb or keto goals, while maintaining high nutritional value. These recipes offer a starting point for crafting meals that support energy, mental clarity, and long-term well-being.

Chapter 10: Additional Resources and Practical Tips

10.1 Smart Grocery Shopping

How to Choose and Buy Healthy and Sustainable Ingredients

Grocery shopping is the foundation of healthy cooking and eating. The choices you make at the store dictate what you'll eat throughout the week, so it's important to approach grocery shopping strategically. In addition to focusing on health, today's shoppers are increasingly concerned with sustainability, choosing ingredients that are both good for their bodies and for the planet. In this chapter, we will explore how to select and buy healthy, sustainable ingredients that align with your nutrition goals while minimizing environmental impact.

1. Planning Ahead for Success

The key to smart grocery shopping is planning. Going to the store without a list or a plan often leads to impulse buys and unhealthy choices. Here are a few steps to set yourself up for success before you even walk through the door:

- Create a Meal Plan: Planning meals in advance helps guide your shopping choices. It ensures that you buy only what you need and reduces food waste. Aim to include a variety of meals that incorporate fresh vegetables, lean proteins, and healthy fats.
- Make a Grocery List: Once you've planned your meals, create a grocery list based on the ingredients you need. Organize your list by categories such as produce, pantry items, proteins, and dairy to make your shopping trip more efficient.
- Check Your Pantry First: Before heading to the store, check what ingredients you already have at home. This avoids overbuying and ensures you use up what's already on hand, reducing waste.
- Shop with a Purpose: Stick to your grocery list to avoid the temptation of unhealthy, processed foods. Supermarkets are designed to encourage impulse purchases, so being disciplined will help you stick to your health and sustainability goals.

2. Choosing Fresh Produce

When it comes to maintaining a healthy diet, fruits and vegetables should make up a significant portion of your grocery haul. Fresh produce is packed with essential vitamins, minerals, and fiber. Here are some tips for selecting the best produce:

- Shop Seasonally: Seasonal produce is often fresher, more flavorful, and more affordable. In-season fruits and vegetables also have a lower environmental impact because they don't require long-distance transportation. For example, berries in the summer and root vegetables in the fall are great seasonal choices.

- Buy Local: Whenever possible, buy from local farmers or farmers' markets. Locally grown produce is not only fresher but also supports local agriculture and reduces the carbon footprint associated with transporting goods across long distances. Look for labels or signs that indicate locally sourced items.
- Organic vs. Conventional: Organic produce is grown without synthetic pesticides or fertilizers, making it a popular choice for those prioritizing health and sustainability. However, organic products can be more expensive. To balance your budget, consider focusing on buying organic for the "Dirty Dozen" – fruits and vegetables that are most likely to have pesticide residue – and opting for conventional versions of the "Clean Fifteen," which tend to have less pesticide residue.

3. Selecting Sustainable Proteins

Protein is an essential part of any diet, whether you are eating animal-based or plant-based foods. However, not all protein sources are equal when it comes to sustainability and health. Here's how to make smarter choices when selecting proteins:

- Choose Lean Meats: Opt for lean cuts of meat like chicken breast, turkey, or fish, which are lower in saturated fats and more heart-friendly. When buying red meat, look for grass-fed beef, which is richer in omega-3 fatty acids and is generally more sustainable than conventionally raised beef.
- Look for Sustainable Seafood: Overfishing and unsustainable fishing practices can harm marine ecosystems. To make environmentally responsible choices, look for seafood that has been certified by organizations like the Marine Stewardship Council (MSC) or the Aquaculture Stewardship Council (ASC). Examples of sustainable seafood include wild-caught Alaskan salmon, sardines, and mussels.
- Plant-Based Proteins: Incorporating more plant-based proteins into your diet, such as beans, lentils, chickpeas, tofu, and tempeh, is a great way to reduce your environmental footprint. Plant-based proteins require fewer natural resources (like water and land) than animal-based proteins and are often more affordable. They are also rich in fiber and low in saturated fat, making them excellent choices for heart health.
- Eggs: Eggs are a highly versatile and nutrient-rich protein source. Look for pasture-raised or organic eggs, which come from hens raised in more humane and sustainable conditions. These eggs tend to have higher levels of omega-3 fatty acids and vitamins compared to conventionally produced eggs.

4. Choosing Grains and Pantry Staples

Grains and pantry items form the backbone of many meals and snacks. When shopping for grains, it's important to focus on whole grains, which offer more nutrients and fiber than refined grains. Here are some tips for selecting healthy, sustainable pantry staples:

- Whole Grains: Choose whole grains like brown rice, quinoa, farro, and barley over refined grains like white rice or pasta. Whole grains contain more fiber, vitamins, and minerals, promoting digestive health and helping to control blood sugar levels.
- Legumes: Beans, lentils, and chickpeas are excellent plant-based proteins and a great source of fiber. Dried legumes are the most cost-effective and have a long shelf life, but canned varieties are also convenient. Look for BPA-free cans, and rinse the legumes before use to reduce sodium.
- Nuts and Seeds: Almonds, walnuts, chia seeds, and flaxseeds are nutrient-dense options that provide healthy fats, protein, and fiber. Buy them in bulk to reduce packaging waste and store them in airtight containers to maintain freshness.
- Flours and Baking Staples: When selecting flours, opt for whole grain or alternative flours like almond flour or coconut flour, which are lower in refined carbohydrates. These flours can be used for baking or cooking and offer additional nutrients compared to traditional white flour.

5. Reading Labels and Avoiding Processed Foods

One of the best ways to ensure you're buying healthy and sustainable ingredients is by reading food labels carefully. Here are some guidelines to help you make informed choices:

- Avoid Ultra-Processed Foods: These are foods that contain artificial ingredients, preservatives, and high levels of sugar, salt, or unhealthy fats. Examples include sugary cereals, snack cakes, chips, and sodas. Instead, opt for minimally processed foods like plain yogurt, whole-grain bread, and canned vegetables without added sodium.
- Check Ingredient Lists: The fewer ingredients, the better. A long list of unpronounceable ingredients often indicates a highly processed product. Look for items with simple, whole-food ingredients.
- Sugar and Sodium: Many packaged foods contain added sugars and sodium. Check for these on the label and choose products with low or no added sugar and minimal sodium content.
- Sustainable Packaging: In addition to the food itself, consider the packaging. Opt for products with minimal or eco-friendly packaging, such as items sold in bulk or those in recyclable materials like glass and cardboard.

6. Shopping Smart for Sustainability

In addition to making healthy food choices, consider how your shopping habits impact the environment. Here are a few tips to reduce your ecological footprint:

- Bring Reusable Bags: Always bring your own reusable shopping bags to reduce plastic waste. Some stores also offer discounts for bringing your own bags.
- Buy in Bulk: Buying dry goods like grains, nuts, and seeds in bulk reduces packaging waste and often saves money. Bring your own containers to the store if possible.

- Reduce Food Waste: Plan meals carefully and avoid buying more than you can consume before items spoil. If you have leftovers or food that's nearing its expiration date, freeze it for later use.

10.2 Meal Preparation and Storage

Techniques for Storing Food and Preparing Meals in Advance

Meal preparation, or meal prep, is a powerful strategy for saving time, reducing stress, and ensuring that you stay on track with healthy eating habits. By preparing meals in advance, you can avoid the temptation of fast food or unhealthy snacks, reduce food waste, and maintain better portion control. Coupled with proper storage techniques, meal prep allows you to enjoy fresh, nutritious meals throughout the week. In this section, we will explore the key techniques for effective meal prep and storage, helping you maximize your time in the kitchen and keep your meals safe and flavorful.

1. The Benefits of Meal Preparation

Meal preparation offers a wide range of benefits, especially for busy individuals looking to maintain a healthy diet. Here are some of the most important advantages:

- Time-saving: By preparing meals in bulk, you save valuable time throughout the week. Instead of cooking multiple times a day, you can simply heat up pre-prepared meals.
- Healthier choices: When meals are prepped in advance, you're less likely to reach for unhealthy, processed foods out of convenience. Having healthy options readily available helps you stay on track with your nutrition goals.
- Portion control: Pre-portioning your meals in advance ensures you eat the right amount of food without overeating or wasting leftovers.
- Cost efficiency: Buying ingredients in bulk and planning meals helps you save money by reducing the need for last-minute takeout or grocery store visits.
- Reduced food waste: With proper planning, you can use all the ingredients you buy, minimizing the chances of unused food spoiling.

2. Meal Preparation Techniques

Effective meal preparation involves more than just cooking in bulk. It requires organization and careful planning to ensure that meals stay fresh and maintain their flavor. Here are some essential meal prep techniques to help you get started:

Batch Cooking
Batch cooking is one of the most efficient ways to meal prep. It involves cooking large portions of food at once, then dividing them into smaller servings for the week. Foods that

are ideal for batch cooking include grains (rice, quinoa, pasta), proteins (chicken, tofu, lentils), and roasted vegetables (carrots, sweet potatoes, broccoli).

- How to Batch Cook: Start by selecting a few key recipes that can be prepared in large quantities. Cook each component (e.g., grains, proteins, vegetables) separately and then combine them in different ways to create a variety of meals. For example, roasted vegetables and grilled chicken can be mixed with quinoa for a salad one day and served in a wrap the next.

Make-Ahead Freezer Meals
Freezing meals is a fantastic way to preserve food for long periods without sacrificing taste or nutrition. Freezer meals can be pre-cooked or pre-assembled and stored in the freezer until you're ready to cook them.

- How to Prep Freezer Meals: Some recipes, like casseroles, soups, or stews, can be fully cooked, cooled, and then frozen in portioned containers. Other dishes, like marinated meats or uncooked stir-fries, can be prepped and frozen raw. When you're ready to eat, thaw the meal in the fridge overnight and then cook or reheat as needed. Make sure to label your containers with the date and contents to keep track of freshness.

Chop and Store Ingredients
Another meal prep technique is to pre-chop vegetables, fruits, and other ingredients in advance. This makes it easy to throw together meals quickly during the week, as the time-consuming prep work has already been done.

- How to Prep Ingredients: Wash, peel, and chop vegetables like carrots, bell peppers, cucumbers, and onions. Store them in airtight containers or resealable bags in the fridge. Leafy greens, such as spinach and kale, can also be prepped by washing and drying them thoroughly, then storing them in airtight containers with a paper towel to absorb excess moisture.

One-Pot or Sheet Pan Meals
One-pot meals and sheet pan dinners are ideal for meal prep because they minimize the number of dishes and streamline the cooking process. These recipes involve cooking everything in one pot or on one sheet pan, making cleanup quick and easy.

- How to Prep One-Pot or Sheet Pan Meals: Combine proteins, vegetables, and spices in a single pot or pan. For example, toss chicken breasts, sweet potatoes, and broccoli with olive oil and seasoning, then roast everything on a sheet pan. After cooking, divide the meal into individual portions for the week.

3. Proper Storage Techniques

Once your meals are prepped, proper storage is crucial to maintain freshness, flavor, and food safety. Different types of foods require specific storage methods to ensure they last as long as possible.

Choose the Right Containers
Investing in high-quality food storage containers is essential for meal prep. Look for containers that are durable, leak-proof, and easy to stack in your fridge or freezer. Glass containers are ideal for reheating food directly in the microwave or oven, while plastic containers are lighter and better for on-the-go meals.

- Airtight Containers: To preserve freshness, always use airtight containers. This prevents moisture loss and keeps food from absorbing odors from the fridge or freezer.
- Portion Sizes: Use different-sized containers to match portion sizes. Smaller containers are great for individual meals or snacks, while larger containers work well for batch-cooked items like grains or proteins.

Label Everything
When storing prepped meals or ingredients, it's essential to label containers with the contents and the date they were prepared. This helps you keep track of what needs to be eaten first and ensures that food doesn't go to waste.

Refrigeration and Freezing Guidelines
Understanding how long different foods last in the fridge or freezer is key to keeping your meals fresh and safe to eat.

- Fridge Storage: Most cooked meals will stay fresh in the refrigerator for 3-4 days. Raw ingredients like pre-chopped vegetables can last for up to a week, but more delicate items like leafy greens may only last a few days.
- Freezer Storage: Cooked meals can be stored in the freezer for 2-3 months. Some ingredients, like soups, stews, and casseroles, freeze exceptionally well, while others, such as raw vegetables, may require blanching before freezing to preserve their texture and nutrients.

Reheating Tips
Reheating prepped meals properly is important for both food safety and taste. When reheating food, ensure it reaches an internal temperature of 165°F (74°C) to kill any bacteria. Avoid reheating food multiple times, as this can cause it to dry out or lose flavor.

- Microwave Reheating: If you're using a microwave to reheat your meals, cover the container with a microwave-safe lid or a damp paper towel to retain moisture.
- Oven or Stovetop Reheating: For meals like casseroles, stir-fries, or roasted vegetables, reheating in the oven or on the stovetop helps maintain the original texture and flavor.

4. Planning for Variety

One of the challenges of meal prep is avoiding monotony. Eating the same meal several days in a row can become tiresome. To keep things interesting, try incorporating different sauces, spices, and sides to transform the same base ingredients into new meals throughout the week.

- Mix and Match Ingredients: Batch-cook ingredients like roasted vegetables, grilled chicken, or quinoa, and mix them with different dressings or seasonings to create unique dishes. For example, roasted vegetables can be added to salads, grain bowls, or wraps, while grilled chicken can be used in stir-fries, tacos, or soups.
- Use Seasonal Ingredients: Incorporating seasonal produce into your meal prep adds variety and ensures that your meals are flavorful and fresh. It also helps you eat more sustainably by choosing ingredients that are in season and locally available.

10.3 Continuous Support for Wellness

Tips for Continuing Your Health Journey After the 28 Days

After completing the 28-day meal plan or initial wellness journey, it can be easy to fall back into old habits. However, the key to long-term success is maintaining momentum and building upon the progress you've made. Wellness is not just a short-term goal; it's a lifestyle that requires ongoing effort, mindfulness, and adaptability. In this section, we'll explore practical tips for continuing your health journey, ensuring that the positive habits you've developed during the 28 days become a lasting part of your daily routine.

1. Embrace Consistency Over Perfection

One of the most important aspects of maintaining a wellness routine is focusing on consistency rather than striving for perfection. It's natural to have days when you deviate from your plan, whether due to social events, travel, or stress. The key is not to feel discouraged or view these moments as failures but to return to your healthy habits as soon as possible.

- Develop Daily Routines: Create daily routines that support your health goals, such as preparing nutritious meals, staying active, and getting enough sleep. These routines will serve as the foundation for your long-term success.
- Allow Flexibility: While it's important to stay committed to your wellness plan, it's also essential to remain flexible. Life is full of unexpected events, and it's important to adapt your health routine to fit your current circumstances. For example, if you can't fit in your usual workout, take a walk or do a quick home exercise.
- Avoid the All-or-Nothing Mentality: If you have an indulgent meal or skip a workout, don't give up on your wellness journey. Instead, refocus on your healthy habits at the next

opportunity. Remember that small, consistent actions are more effective over time than trying to be perfect every day.

2. Set New Goals

Once you've completed the initial 28-day plan, it's helpful to set new, achievable goals to keep you motivated. These goals can be related to any area of wellness, including nutrition, fitness, mental health, or personal growth.

- Break Larger Goals Into Small Steps: Large, long-term goals can feel overwhelming, so break them down into smaller, manageable steps. For example, if your goal is to eat more plant-based meals, start by incorporating one or two plant-based dinners per week, then gradually increase.
- Track Your Progress: Whether through a journal, an app, or regular check-ins with a friend or coach, tracking your progress helps you stay accountable and motivated. It also allows you to reflect on your successes and identify areas where you can improve.
- Celebrate Milestones: As you achieve your goals, celebrate those milestones! Acknowledging your progress, no matter how small, keeps you motivated to continue your wellness journey.

3. Continue Exploring New Foods and Recipes

One of the most exciting aspects of a wellness journey is discovering new foods, flavors, and recipes. To keep things interesting, continue experimenting with different ingredients, cuisines, and cooking techniques.

- Try New Recipes Weekly: To avoid falling into a food rut, aim to try one or two new recipes each week. This will keep your meals fresh and exciting, and help you discover new favorite dishes. Incorporate seasonal produce and experiment with different cuisines to broaden your culinary horizons.
- Make Healthy Substitutions: As you continue your wellness journey, look for healthy swaps that can elevate your meals. For example, use zucchini noodles instead of pasta, cauliflower rice instead of white rice, or Greek yogurt instead of sour cream. These substitutions allow you to enjoy your favorite meals while keeping them nutritious.
- Meal Prep for Success: Continue meal prepping to save time and stay on track. Whether it's preparing ingredients in advance, batch cooking, or freezing meals, meal prep ensures that you always have healthy options available, even on busy days.

4. Stay Active and Enjoy Your Workouts

Regular physical activity is a cornerstone of long-term wellness. However, to maintain an active lifestyle, it's important to find exercises you enjoy. Forcing yourself to do workouts you dislike can lead to burnout and discourage consistency. Instead, focus on activities that make you feel energized and happy.

- Mix Up Your Routine: Keep your workouts varied by trying different types of exercise, such as strength training, yoga, cycling, swimming, or hiking. This not only prevents boredom but also challenges your body in new ways, leading to improved fitness and strength.
- Set Fitness Goals: Just like with nutrition, setting fitness goals helps you stay motivated. Whether it's increasing the number of push-ups you can do, running a 5K, or mastering a yoga pose, having specific goals encourages you to push yourself and track your progress.
- Incorporate Movement Into Daily Life: Staying active doesn't always mean going to the gym. Find small ways to incorporate movement into your daily life, such as taking the stairs, going for a walk after meals, or stretching while watching TV. These small actions add up over time and contribute to your overall wellness.

5. Prioritize Mental and Emotional Well-Being

Wellness is not just about physical health; it also includes mental and emotional well-being. Continuing your health journey means taking care of your mind as much as your body. Incorporating mindfulness, stress management, and self-care practices into your routine can greatly enhance your overall sense of wellness.

- Practice Mindfulness: Mindfulness is the practice of being present in the moment without judgment. It can reduce stress, improve focus, and promote emotional balance. Try incorporating mindfulness techniques like meditation, deep breathing, or journaling into your daily routine.
- Manage Stress: Chronic stress can negatively impact both physical and mental health. Find healthy ways to manage stress, whether through exercise, spending time in nature, practicing gratitude, or engaging in creative hobbies like painting, writing, or gardening.
- Seek Support When Needed: Don't hesitate to reach out for support when you need it. Whether it's talking to a friend, joining a wellness group, or seeking professional counseling, having a support system is essential for maintaining mental and emotional well-being.

6. Stay Informed and Adapt

As you continue your wellness journey, it's important to stay informed about new research, trends, and practices in nutrition, fitness, and overall health. Being open to learning and adapting your habits can help you fine-tune your routine for long-term success.

- Keep Learning: Read books, listen to podcasts, and follow reputable wellness experts to stay up-to-date with the latest information. This can help you incorporate new ideas and practices into your routine.
- Listen to Your Body: Pay attention to how your body responds to different foods, workouts, and self-care practices. Everyone's wellness journey is unique, and what works

for someone else may not be the best approach for you. Adjust your routine as needed to suit your evolving needs.

7. Create a Supportive Environment

Finally, building a supportive environment is essential for long-term success. Surround yourself with people who encourage your wellness goals and create a home environment that fosters healthy habits.

- Involve Friends and Family: Share your wellness journey with friends and family and invite them to join you in activities like cooking healthy meals together or going for a walk. Having a support network keeps you accountable and motivated.
- Keep Your Kitchen Stocked: Continue to stock your kitchen with nutritious ingredients. Having healthy foods on hand makes it easier to prepare balanced meals and avoid unhealthy temptations.

Conclusion

Continuing your health journey after the initial 28-day plan is all about consistency, adaptability, and self-compassion. By setting new goals, staying active, exploring new foods, and prioritizing mental well-being, you can maintain the momentum and make wellness a sustainable part of your life. Remember that wellness is a lifelong journey, and with the right strategies and mindset, you can continue to grow and thrive in the months and years to come.

Made in the USA
Las Vegas, NV
25 October 2024